PERSONAL BANKRUPTCY AND DEBT ADJUSTMENT

A STEP-BY-STEP GUIDE

PERSONAL BANKRUPTCY AND DEBT ADJUSTMENT

Second Edition

A STEP-BY-STEP GUIDE

KENNETH J. DORAN

RANDOM HOUSE  NEW YORK

An earlier edition of this work was published in 1991 by Random House, Inc.

Library of Congress Cataloging-in-Publication Data

Doran, Kenneth J.
    Personal bankruptcy and debt adjustment : a step-by-
    step guide / Kenneth J. Doran. — 2nd ed.
      p. cm.
    ISBN: 0-679-76976-5 (pbk. : alk. paper)
    1. Bankruptcy — United States — Popular works.
    I. Title.
    KF1524.6.D67   1996
    346.73'078 — dc20   95-44479
    [347.30678]   CIP

Book design by Charlotte Staub

Typeset and Printed in the United States of America

Second Edition

9 8 7 6 5 4 3 2 1

New York Toronto London Sydney Auckland

*For Dianne, Taylor and Olivia; and for
Alice Doran*

Acknowledgments

I gratefully acknowledge the support of my family and particularly my wife, Dianne. I also want to express my appreciation for the assistance of: Ronald M. Legro and Constance Kilmark, who read the manuscript of the first edition and provided valuable comments; my agent Oscar Collier; the people at Random House; the dozens of lawyers and judges who have provided lessons in law and the operation of the legal system; and, most important, the thousands of people who have done me the honor of seeking out my advice and assistance and who, I fervently hope, have benefited from it. The responsibility for any errors is entirely mine.

Kenneth J. Doran

Contents

Introduction

PRESIDENT SIGNS "FRESH START" LAW

WASHINGTON—Congress has passed and the President signed a financial fresh start law.

The law provides for cancellation on request of many kinds of debts for people who can't meet their financial obligations. Under the new law, a debt cancellation request in federal court immediately suspends lawsuits, wage garnishments, and other debt collection, even before a judge rules on the request.

Many filers under the law will be able to keep all property that has not been mortgaged or pledged as collateral, free and clear of creditors' claims. In addition, the law completely or partially frees up some types of property that have been used as collateral and would otherwise be subject to repossession.

Some debts that cannot be canceled outright under the law, including back taxes and mortgage defaults, can be dealt with through debt adjustment plans. The Internal Revenue Service and other creditors are forbidden to take any debt collection steps while payments are being made through the court.

Estimates of filings under the law are expected to be
(continued)

How would you react if you saw that story in your newspaper? Would you be outraged that people might avoid paying their legal debts? Or pleased that there is a way out from under oppressive debts for those who need it?

The story is true and it isn't really news. People who are in debt do have all these rights and more under federal law. And that situation didn't come about suddenly or recently. Most of the "fresh start law" has been on the books for fifty to a hundred years.

Why is this remarkable law so little known and understood? The reasons have something to do with the ominous ring the law's name has for many people. That name is bankruptcy. The fresh start law is the United States Bankruptcy Code.

The word "bankruptcy" is used and misused in a lot of ways. Properly applied, "bankrupt" doesn't mean "broke" or "in debt." Bankruptcy is a process for *dealing* with serious debt problems. It is more like a treatment than an illness.

When I started handling bankruptcy cases as a lawyer, I noticed a surprising pattern among the people who came to see me about it. Many of them started out by asking, "Now, just what is bankruptcy, anyway?" This, mind you, from people who had at least figured out that bankruptcy might help them and gotten as far as seeing a lawyer about it. Clients who came for other things also had some very basic questions, but few needed to know what, for example, a divorce or will is.

It didn't take me long to start wondering: If even the people who come to see a lawyer about bankruptcy know so little about it, how many others out there never even investigate their rights—because they don't know there is anything to look for?

In seventeen years as a lawyer I have helped more than twelve hundred people file bankruptcies or debt adjustment plans. I have advised at least that many others who decided to handle their financial problems in other ways. I have also represented creditors on the other side of the table in bankruptcy court. Along the way, I have learned a great deal about both the theoretical and practical sides of bankruptcy law. And I still wonder how many people forfeit their legal options because they don't even know they should look for them.

Many people—perhaps most—know little or nothing about their legal fresh start rights. And those who think they know something are as likely as not to be badly mistaken. Filing bankruptcy does not mean "you will never get credit again" or "they'll take everything you've got" or "they'll come out and search your house."

Of course, no one is happy about filing for bankruptcy, but I'm convinced that the dread sound of the word keeps many people from investigating and asserting important legal rights.

Some of the reasons for this are historical. Attitudes survive from a small-town era when debts were more likely to be true person-to-person obligations. If you owe money to a friend or the corner grocer, the burden of not paying in full will feel worse than if you owe a credit card balance. Also, the "credit industry" of banks, finance companies, and others tries to maintain vague fears and apprehensions surrounding bankruptcy. They use the same approach with credit ratings, as if you will never recover from credit problems. I'm not so sure this is really in their interest, but they think it is.

My hope for this book is to build a bridge. I have tried to start from a point that assumes as little as possible and move to a useful general understanding of the bankruptcy law and process. I assume that many readers will be people who have at least some reason to believe they may have need of these laws. I hope this book will give them a chance to evaluate their situation in privacy, before taking the understandably difficult step of discussing their financial problems with an outsider.

I have tried to use lay terms and explain necessary legal concepts as we go along. There is also a glossary at the end of the book.

I also hope the book will be useful to people coming into

contact with bankruptcy from any direction, as well as to general readers seeking an understanding of this particular corner of our legal and economic systems.

Kenneth J. Doran
Madison, Wisconsin
July, 1995

PERSONAL BANKRUPTCY AND DEBT ADJUSTMENT

A STEP-BY-STEP GUIDE

CHAPTER 1

WHAT IS BANKRUPTCY?

The short answer to "What is bankruptcy?" is that it is a set of legal procedures for dealing with debt problems of individuals and businesses.

The long answer is the rest of this book.

About 833,000 bankruptcy cases were filed in the United States in 1994. At the current rate, about one American in ten will file some type of bankruptcy case during his or her life.

POVERTY AND DEBT PROBLEMS

Having debt problems is not the same thing as being poor; the two can certainly go together, but they don't necessarily. There are people with incomes well above average, with nice homes and cars, who are nevertheless swamped by more debts than they can handle. Now and then we hear of a bankruptcy filing by a highly paid executive, entertainer, or athlete. On the other hand, some people with low incomes and very modest lifestyles are financially stable and don't owe anyone a nickel.

Neither a bankruptcy nor a debt adjustment plan can directly increase your income or fatten your bank account. They very likely can free you in whole or in part from unmanageable debts and give you a financial fresh start. If your problem is accumulated debts, bankruptcy or debt adjustment may be able to make a difference for you. If your problem is something else—for example a lower income than what you need or want—these laws probably won't do you any good.

The way you get into bankruptcy court is by filing a petition for protection under the law. Bankruptcy is nearly always "voluntary" in the sense that the person filing has to agree to it, although as a practical matter there is often little choice.

Before a bankruptcy case is over, a court order usually cancels at least some—and possibly all—of the debts of the person who files. In formal bankruptcy terminology, the debts are "discharged," and the court order that does it is called a "discharge in bankruptcy."

A person filing for a discharge used to be known officially as a "bankrupt." Since the 1970s the formal term has been "debtor" or sometimes "petitioner," the term most often used in this book.

WHAT HAPPENS IN BANKRUPTCY

In some bankruptcy cases, part of the petitioner's property is sold and the proceeds used to pay a portion of the petitioner's debts. This happens in relatively few cases, perhaps as few as one out of twenty in some states. Most of the time, the petitioner's property is *not* sold because people who file for bankruptcy usually don't have enough property for creditors to bother with.

Even when the petitioner does have some property, part or all of it is protected. It may be tied up by liens and mortgages that pledge it to specific creditors. These "protect" the property from *other* creditors and from the trustee who represents them in the bankruptcy. Whether that protection does the petitioner much good depends on the circumstances, as we will see later.

Certain additional property is protected because it is legally classified as "exempt," a term we will discuss. The petitioner can keep exempt property even while receiving a discharge of debts.

Between those two categories—exempt property and property with liens—there is often nothing left to be sold in the bankruptcy for the "unsecured" creditors, the ones who don't have liens.

WHO CAN FILE FOR BANKRUPTCY?

There are few restrictions on who can file for bankruptcy. No minimum dollar amount of debts is required, but there is a time limit on *repeat* bankruptcies. For six years after receiving a bankruptcy discharge, that petitioner cannot get another one. Other than that, almost anyone who has serious debt problems and needs the protection of bankruptcy law can apply.

Even with a bankruptcy less than six years old on record, a person may be able to obtain some protection from creditors. It may still be possible to file under the "debt adjustment" or payback section of the law, known as Chapter 13, before the six years are up (see page 37).

A SHORT HISTORY OF BANKRUPTCY

Critics of bankruptcy often give the impression that it is a new invention. There have been some important changes in the law in recent years, but there is nothing new about the basic principles.

As long ago as Old Testament times, there was something

parallel to bankruptcy; Chapter 15 of the Book of Deuteron-
omy calls for the release of all debts every seven years.
Ancient Roman law also had a form of bankruptcy.

Bankruptcy as we know it today traces its history to laws
passed in England in 1542 under King Henry VIII. Like most
elements of our legal system, bankruptcy laws were brought
to America by English colonists.

The word "bankruptcy" comes from Italian words mean-
ing "broken bench." By one early custom, when a merchant
or tradesman could not pay his debts, his workbench or
display table in the marketplace was broken as a symbol of
his failure.

In 1787 the authors of the U.S. Constitution made specific
provisions for bankruptcy that continue in effect today. The
Constitution gives authority over bankruptcy to the federal
government. A special branch of the federal courts handles
bankruptcy cases, officially known as petitions under Title 11
of the United States Code. The separate state court systems
deal with most related legal matters, such as small claims,
foreclosures, and general debt collection lawsuits.

THE BANKRUPTCY DISCHARGE
AND THE FRESH START

What is bankruptcy *for*?

Opinions on that may vary, but Congress and the Supreme
Court are the people who ought to know. They have often
described it in upbeat terms that contrast with the dire
image many people have of bankruptcy.

Specifically, they have said that bankruptcy is a means to
give debtors a financial "fresh start." The Supreme Court
used that description as long ago as 1885. One of their clear-
est and simplest statements on the point was made in a 1934
decision. The justices said that the purpose of the bankruptcy law was to give:

the honest but unfortunate debtor . . . a new opportunity in life and a clear field for future effort, unhampered by the pressure and discouragement of preexisting debt.[1]

THE BANKRUPTCY COURTS

The bankruptcy courts have their own judges and offices and are set up in the same system of "districts" as other federal courts. Each state has one or more districts, and many districts are divided into two or more divisions. A personal bankruptcy petition must be filed in the district where the petitioner lives or operates a business.

TYPES OF BANKRUPTCY CASES: THE "CHAPTERS"

There are several different types of bankruptcy cases, usually referred to by the chapters of the Bankruptcy Code that provide for them. This book deals mostly with "Liquidation" (Chapter 7) and "Adjustment of Debts of an Individual with Regular Income" (Chapter 13).

CHAPTER 7

Chapter 7, also known as "straight bankruptcy," is the simplest and most basic type of case. Its official name refers to the process of "liquidating" property—selling it off for cash to apply to the petitioner's debts.

Despite that title, no property is actually "liquidated" in most cases. A lot of property, sometimes everything a petitioner has, cannot legally be taken because it is, as we discussed, either tied up by liens or classified as exempt.

---

[1]*Local Loan v. Hunt, 292 U.S. 234, 245 (1934)*

The only significant result of most Chapter 7 cases is the discharge or cancellation of at least some of the petitioner's debts. A Chapter 7 petitioner does not have to make payments out of his or her future income on debts that have been discharged.

For details of the uses, advantages, and disadvantages of Chapter 7 bankruptcy, see Chapter 5.

CHAPTER 13

In a Chapter 13 debt adjustment case, the petitioner does not ask for an immediate discharge of debts. Instead, he or she offers a "plan" to pay off at least part of those debts over time—usually three years, though it can be as long as five years. The petitioner is protected from lawsuits, garnishments, and other creditor action while the plan is in effect.

"Wage earner bankruptcy" and "wage earner plan" are outdated terms for what is now Chapter 13. A Chapter 13 petitioner must have a regular income, but it can be from any source, not just wages.

For details of the uses, advantages, and disadvantages of Chapter 13 debt adjustment, see Chapter 5.

THE OTHER CHAPTERS OF
THE BANKRUPTCY CODE

There are several other sections of the Bankruptcy Code that are not covered to any extent in this book. "Business Reorganization" (Chapter 11) and "Family Farm Reorganization" (Chapter 12) are similar to Chapter 13 but more complicated. Chapter 9 applies to cities, counties, and other governmental units that default on their debts. There are special sections of the law for railroads and stockbrokers.

Yet another section covers the U.S. property and operations of companies that are in bankruptcy or similar proceedings in other countries.

U.S. law also allows *creditors* to file an involuntary bankruptcy petition *against* a debtor. This forces into bankruptcy a person or business that has not filed voluntarily. Involuntary bankruptcies are uncommon, and almost all are filed against businesses. It is legally possible to file one against a consumer or wage earner, but it is very rare.

HOW MANY PEOPLE ARE AFFECTED?

In 1994, about 833,000 bankruptcy cases of all types were filed in the United States. About 93 percent of those cases, more than 778,000, were nonbusiness Chapter 7's and Chapter 13's, basically the consumer cases. And of those, about 69 percent were Chapter 7's, though the ratio varies widely from one place to another. Approximately two thirds of the Chapter 13's are eventually dropped or changed into Chapter 7's.

In past years about 43 percent of Chapter 7's and 13's were joint husband-and-wife filings. Using that figure, we can estimate that more than 1,100,000 individual Americans filed for consumer bankruptcy or Chapter 13 in 1994.

THE REALITIES OF DEBT PROBLEMS

In a perfect world, no one would never get into debt beyond his or her ability to pay—or enter an unsuccessful marriage, fall afoul of drugs or alcohol, or make a the wrong career choice. In the real world, things like that do happen.

How do people get too far into debt? Every bankruptcy is different. Most have more than one cause, and though no two result from exactly the same combination of problems, some of the same factors turn up time after time. At least one of these is involved in nearly all cases:

Unemployment   The simplest route to financial trouble: You lose your job, your income plummets, and manageable debts become unmanageable.

Illness or Injury   Medical care is expensive. Some health insurance policies are better than others, and some people have no insurance at all. If a wage earner misses work beyond his or her sick benefits, that loss of income is a further drain on the family's finances.

Divorce or Separation   An income that was adequate for one household often isn't enough for two. Meeting the increased current expenses may not leave enough money for payment of debts. One spouse or both may end up in bankruptcy.

Business Failure   Chasing the dream of being your own boss is risky. A high percentage of small businesses fail, and the owner is often left with large debts.

Poor Planning   Some people—but probably not as many as you might think—get into trouble by careless or poorly planned use of credit. Too many "easy" payments out of a family's income can be anything but easy to make.

ABUSE OF THE LAW

Not every bankruptcy petitioner necessarily has a good reason for filing or a real need for a fresh start. For a few, bankruptcy may just be an easy way out of debts they could pay if they wanted to.

If it is possible for a right or privilege to be abused, it will sometimes happen. There is no reason to imagine that bankruptcy would be totally immune from such abuse, and it isn't. But there is also little evidence that such abuse is common. Since 1984, judges have been able to throw out some bankruptcy cases that are a "substantial abuse" of the law. They have rarely done so, which suggests that the problem is not widespread.

Those few people who do misuse bankruptcy are probably far outnumbered by people in just the opposite situation—people who have exactly the debt problems that Congress intended bankruptcy to solve and who never get that help because they don't have the information they need.

WHAT TRIGGERS BANKRUPTCY

Sometimes a particular event in a person's life triggers an interest in the possibility of bankruptcy. There is, however, no strong pattern. Some people decide they are overextended and headed for serious trouble even before they have actually missed a single payment. Others don't act until they have been through repeated lawsuits and wage garnishments. Most petitioners fall somewhere in between.

Lawsuits, foreclosures, and wage garnishments are often alarming, but debt collection outside of court can have just as much effect. When you owe money, collection letters and telephone calls can feel overwhelming—even before your creditors go to court. If the burden of dealing with collection is damaging your life, relieving that burden is as good a reason as any for filing bankruptcy.

In a way, the decision to investigate and file for bankruptcy is a choice between two sets of stresses—the all-too-familiar stresses of debt problems, and the unknown ones that might be found in the bankruptcy process. Our hope in this book is to reduce that fear of the unknown and open the way to making clear and careful decisions about these important matters.

CHAPTER 2

THREE STORIES

The people you are about to meet are imaginary, but writing their stories didn't take much imagination. Fragments of these tales appear in almost every bankruptcy case.

We will meet this cast of characters again in later sections of this book, as we use their stories to illustrate the workings of the bankruptcy laws.

Thomas Martinez made a lot of progress toward the American dream, and he did it the old-fashioned way. After high school he worked at a variety of jobs, from selling shirts to cleaning carpets. At twenty-two he began to do construction work, and by twenty-five he was working regularly and getting an impressive hourly wage. There were some slow-season layoffs, but Tom was making almost as much as his father did as a high school teacher with thirty years' experience.

By twenty-eight, Tom was married to Sandy, a salesclerk, and they had two children. Sandy had cut back to half-time work to spend more time with the children. Even so, between the two of them, they managed to pay the rent, buy the groceries, and make the payments on a car and some furniture.

Sandy and Tom used credit cards to smooth out the hills and valleys of their income. They charged various expenses in the slow times and paid off the balances when Tom was working steadily. In time they had five different credit cards, and they could have had ten more just by sending back the applications that came in the mail.

After several good years, the construction industry slumped. Tom found himself working only six months of the year instead of the ten or eleven he was used to. The immediate impact on the Martinez family was not that great—except for their credit card balances. The totals went up and stayed up. They used the cards for clothes, shoes, and other purchases, and sometimes for cash advances as well. Paying the balances became a lot harder than it had been.

One year like that, Tom and Sandy could have taken more or less in stride. Three in a row, each a little worse than the last, were a different matter. Tom's construction income continued to drop, and his unemployment compensation and fill-in jobs didn't make up the difference. Though Sandy went back to work full time, in the depressed job market she couldn't get much more than minimum wage.

The rising credit card bills were joined by a finance company loan at an even higher rate of interest. After a while, Tom and Sandy couldn't make even the minimum payments on the accounts.

Collection letters and telephone calls began, starting as a trickle and building to a flood. A couple of times, process servers showed up at the door with particularly serious-looking papers having to do with some of the bills. Tom couldn't pay, and so, not knowing what else to do, he ignored the papers. It seemed to work; nothing bad happened.

The run of bad luck had just about broken Tom and Sandy's resolve—and then things turned around. The construction business picked up. Sandy got a promotion. They started paying off some of the debts. For a couple of months, Tom was making more money than he ever had.

Then one of the credit card companies filed a wage garnishment. Those papers Tom had ignored were lawsuits, and a credit card company had won an uncontested court judgment against him. Because of that, the company was allowed to deduct 25 percent of Tom's take-home pay.

Just about then, Sandy moved out and sued Tom for divorce. The marriage had been over for a long time, she told him. She had waited only because she had not wanted to hurt him when he was already down.

Susan Novak had all the brains and determination it took to go to college and get a degree. What she didn't have was the money, but she didn't allow that to stop her.

Her mother helped when she could, but with two other children in high school, she couldn't do very much. Sue worked part time and summers, as she had since she was fifteen, but even at a state university, her income wasn't enough. She applied for financial aid and qualified for work-study eligibility, some small scholarship grants, and loans—quite a number of loans.

Neither Sue nor her mother liked the idea of borrowing thousands of dollars every year. The advisers at the college, on the other hand, didn't seem too concerned. They told Sue that she wouldn't have to pay anything until nine months after she graduated, that the interest wouldn't start accruing until then, and that she could take up to ten years to pay, at a low interest rate subsidized by the government.

Sue's choice was clear. She could delay her ambition of graduating from college, or she could take the loans and worry about the payments later. By the time she had to pay, she would surely have a good job.

Four years later, Sue had a degree in English with honors, a desire to be a fiction writer, and hopes of going to graduate school. She also had $15,000 in student loans. Since a master's degree would have entailed even more loans, she decided to try the job market for a while. Since she had no illusions about making a quick killing as a novelist, she took the best job she could find, as a loan officer trainee in a bank.

Within two years, Sue had earned a promotion and made the first five quarterly payments on her student loans. By then, having written some short stories and saved a little money, she was also chafing at her job. It wasn't unbearable, but it was keeping her from her true calling—writing.

When Sue sold three of her stories to magazines, she decided to make the break and try to write full time. She knew it was a gamble because what she got paid for a story was less than she made in a week at the bank. Taking the view that life is a gamble, Sue handed in her resignation.

Six months later, the gamble showed some signs of paying off. Sue had sold five more stories. To avoid using up her savings too fast, she worked part time as a free-lance editor and a waitress. One weekend she followed twenty-four straight hours of writing with four hours of waitressing. She got through her shift and made it home. Halfway up the stairs, fatigue got the better of her and she missed a step and bounced ten steps back down. It turned out she had injured her neck and back. The aches and pains held on through months of return visits to the doctor, physical therapy, a brief hospital stay—and lots of medical bills.

Those bills brought Sue eye to eye with a decision she had made when she quit the bank. Because the restaurant didn't offer health insurance and private insurance was too expensive, Sue had decided to take a chance without it. It was one gamble she lost.

Sue's savings disappeared quickly, and though the doctor and the hospital didn't turn her away, they did bill her several thousand dollars. When she didn't pay—as she couldn't—they put collection agencies on the case.

The pain from Sue's physical problems also interfered with her writing, and that helped push her to a painful decision. She went back to work full time at the bank.

Her health improved to the point where it didn't interfere significantly with her bank work. Unfortunately, her debt problems didn't show the same improvement. Besides the medical bills, there were some smaller debts that she had built up in her low-income days. Debt collectors called her at home and interrupted her at work, and they were usually not very sympathetic.

Sue had also stopped paying the student loan, and for some time she was surprised that she didn't hear from anyone about it. Eventually the student loan agency notified Sue that she owed more than $14,000, including interest. Since she was in default on the payments, the full amount was due immediately. Sue tried to work out an agreement with the agency to start paying again at a rate she could afford. She got nowhere.

Eight months after Sue returned to the bank, within three days of each other, the student loan agency and the hospital both filed lawsuits against her.

Dave and Beth Wilson didn't just jump into starting a business. And it wasn't something they had to do. They both had good jobs, Dave as a building inspector and Beth as a secretary. They were able to make payments on a home and keep their two children in food and clothes.

But they had bigger dreams. To Dave and Beth, independence and success meant being their own bosses—owning a business. Dave had worked in sporting goods stores for several years during and after college. The Wilsons decided that sporting goods would be their best shot at going into business.

After looking for almost two years, they bought a small suburban store from its owner, who was retiring. They put up $15,000 from their savings as a down payment and agreed to pay $85,000 more over seven years.

From the start the Wilsons planned to move the business into a new shopping center in a growing residential area, and in six months they did it. Dave quit his job to manage the store, and Beth worked evenings and weekends keeping the books. The business grew, and within a year they moved again, to a larger spot in the same shopping center. Things were going well enough that Beth also quit her job to work in the business full time.

The next few years were even better. The Wilsons qualified for their first bank loan. They used the money to pay what they owed the former owner and to open a smaller second store. The business was going so well that they no longer had to do as much belt tightening as they had at first. They were paying themselves more than they had earned in their old jobs.

The Wilsons considered themselves successful, with good reason. They worked long hours, but they rewarded themselves with some of the things they had never been able to afford. They bought the two most expensive cars they had ever owned and a camper they rarely used—they didn't feel comfortable leaving the store for long trips. Finally they started building their dream home.

The thriving area in which the Wilsons had opened their store was a good choice. It was so good that the owners of a lot of other businesses, large and small, eventually decided they liked it too. Within the space of a year, another sporting goods store, a department store, and a large discount store—all connected to regional or national chains—opened within a mile of Dave and Beth's main location. The competition hurt: Instead of recording higher sales every month as they had come to expect, Dave and Beth experienced drops of 20 to 30 percent from the previous year.

Because they had been putting their profits back into the business, they did not have much cash put aside to deal with the downturn. Payments on the bank loan left them stretched thin financially, but when they tried to get an additional loan their bank refused them.

The Wilsons remained confident that they could turn the business around. Their shopping center was planning a major expansion that would make it the main focus of retail activity in the area for years to come. Dave and Beth were sure the new development would put them back on top. The challenge was to stay in business long enough for it to happen.

They cut their own salaries; in a small business, the owner gets paid last. They laid off some of their employees—including Beth, who went back to work as a secretary.

Then they started "stretching out" some of their bills. First they delayed payments due to the government for taxes withheld from employees' paychecks. Then they started falling behind on payments to their suppliers. Some suppliers got very cranky about it very fast; a few others hardly seemed to notice. Dave cut his own salary again, and the Wilson household finances suffered seriously.

In time Beth and Dave had to close the second store. For the first time since starting in business, they began falling behind on the store rent and bank loan payments. They stopped paying themselves altogether. One creditor filed a lawsuit. Then five more did.

Only the payroll remained sacred; no employee of D&B Sports Center—except Dave—ever missed a paycheck.

A week before the groundbreaking on the shopping center expansion that was to be Dave and Beth's salvation, the center's owners announced that their financing had fallen through. Within days, the two largest stores in the center announced plans to close.

Dave and Beth knew that D&B Sports Center was finished, and that it was leaving them with some very big problems. They also realized that in their entire time in business, they had never really thought about just what would happen—or what they would do—if that day ever came.

CHAPTER **3**

WHO FILES FOR BANKRUPTCY?

Thomas Martinez, Susan Novak, and the Wilsons are not unique either in their troubles or in their way of life. More than a million Americans file for bankruptcy each year. Who are they? Where do they come from?

Official statistics tell us very little. The best figures available come from the efforts of Professors Teresa Sullivan, Lawrence Westbrook and Elizabeth Warren. In 1981 they organized the Consumer Bankruptcy Project, the largest and most thorough information-gathering and analysis project in the history of American bankruptcy law. Their findings were published in 1989 in the book *As We Forgive Our Debtors.*

A brief review of some of their key findings follows. When looking at the specific dollar amounts, remember that these numbers are from 1981. Comparable figures fifteen years later would be 60 to 70 percent higher.

INCOME LEVELS

For the country as a whole in 1981, a midlevel family had an income of $22,400. The midlevel bankruptcy filer had a family income of about $15,000. That many bankruptcy petitioners have low incomes is no surprise. There is a lot of overlap, however. Nearly one petitioner in four came from a family with a *higher* income than the majority of his or her fellow citizens.

OCCUPATION

About 23 percent of petitioners were in professional-technical or manager-administrator occupations. That compares with 35 percent of the general population in those categories. Several job categories showed up more often among bankruptcy petitioners. These included craftspeople, transport workers, general laborers, and service workers.

In terms of the type of business or employer for which they worked, the petitioners again tended to have a profile similar to that of the general population. A few more people than average came from transportation and retail industries and the military. Relatively small numbers reported jobs in construction, wholesale, and professional services.

THE SELF-EMPLOYED

Business owners in particular are in danger of ending up in bankruptcy. More than 20 percent of petitioners were in business for themselves or had been in the recent past. In the country as a whole, only 7.3 percent were in that category.

The financial data of business owners showed significant differences from those of wage earners. The self-employed tended to have more assets, often including business equipment or inventory. However, that was more than offset by higher debts.

Finding so many business owners in personal bankruptcy runs counter to the common notion that business bankruptcy and personal bankruptcy are two entirely different things. In reality they are often bound together in a single individual's situation.

Small businesses have a high failure rate, and the owner or owners are usually left with significant debts. This is particularly true of someone who has been sole owner of a business or a partner in it. In both of those situations, any debt of the business is also a personal debt of the owner or partners.

When the business is set up as a corporation, the owners are protected from having to pay some kinds of debts of the business. This so-called "limited liability" is one of the major reasons for incorporating a business. However, the owners can still be liable when they have personally guaranteed debts of the business, when payroll or sales taxes have not been paid, and in some other situations.

HOMEOWNERS

Slightly more than half of bankruptcy filers reported owning their own homes, compared with 64 percent for the country as a whole. The reported values of their homes were less than those of the general population, but not significantly. As with business owners, homeowners have both higher total assets and more debts than others.

MEDICAL DEBT

For all bankruptcy petitioners, medical debts made up 11 percent of nonmortgage debt. Not surprisingly, the distribution was uneven. About half of the cases showed no medical debt at all, while a few reported crushing amounts.

Those figures include only actual medical bills; they don't reflect reduced income or increased expenses incidental to an illness.

WHO ARE THE CREDITORS?

The Bankruptcy Project found the following major categories of creditors to whom petitioners owed money:

Type of Creditor	Percentage of Debt
Banks	24
Stores	14
Savings and loans	11
Finance companies—nonauto	10
Private mortgage companies	10
Finance companies—auto	3
Credit unions	3
Medical care providers	2
Taxes	2
Gasoline credit cards	2
Other	19
Total	100

These percentages can't be used to explain which creditors are most at risk of not getting paid. Some are much
better protected by collateral on their accounts than others.
Savings and loans, private mortgage companies, and car
finance companies are almost totally protected by their
rights to take property. At the other end of the spectrum,
stores, medical providers, and gasoline companies have virtually no such protection.

These findings only hint at the variety of situations that
turn up in bankruptcy court. And though some individuals
come close to matching the general picture, most petitioners
have their own peculiar combination of financial grief.

Bankruptcy petitioners are a lot like the rest of the people
in the world in every way but that one critical point—problem debt situations that cause them to use their rights under
the bankruptcy laws.

CHAPTER 4

CHOOSING A BANKRUPTCY LAWYER

Do you need a lawyer to file for bankruptcy?

You can legally file for bankruptcy or Chapter 13 without a lawyer, and some people do it. I don't recommend it—and not just because I make my living as a bankruptcy lawyer.

WHAT YOU NEED A LAWYER FOR

First, bankruptcy law and the related laws are technical and complex, and there are many variations, exceptions, and possible complications. A good bankruptcy lawyer knows what they are. Many cases turn out to be routine and uncomplicated, especially under Chapter 7, but even a specialist can't tell for certain in advance which ones will turn out to be more complex.

Second, the forms that must be filed with the Bankruptcy Court are not well designed for use by a nonlawyer. They are not self-explanatory and don't come with good instructions.

Third, a lawyer can be a friendly guide through uncharted territory. Even if you feel confident about handling the court hearing and negotiating with creditors on your own, be sure you are fully prepared before getting yourself into that situation.

Whether you have a lawyer or not, you should become as familiar as possible with the procedure to help you judge whether things are going well and to keep track of your affairs. This knowledge will help you make better use of a lawyer.

DOING YOUR OWN BANKRUPTCY

There are several do-your-own-bankruptcy books on the market. If you are determined to do your own bankruptcy, it is probably worth your while to read at least one. Look for a recent copyright date; the laws and forms change often. Unfortunately, I know of no book I can wholeheartedly recommend.

In general, doing your own bankruptcy is something like doing your own plumbing or engine overhaul. If you have a pretty good idea of what you are doing and don't run into any unexpected complications, you can save some money. If things do go wrong, you can easily end up spending more and going through more trouble than if you had hired a specialist to begin with. You should read this book before you contact a lawyer so that you can get the most out of your association and evaluate his or her advice. But this book is not a substitute for a bankruptcy lawyer.

PAYING THE FEES

How can someone who is going bankrupt afford legal fees? Some lawyers ask for payment in advance, but others will wait to receive some or all of their fees until after you have filed with the court. This is more common if you file a Chapter 13 debt adjustment, where the lawyer can often be paid through the court, out of the same money that will be passed on to other creditors. In Chapter 7 cases, there is usually no money available through the court from which the lawyer can be paid.

As we have seen, most people who find themselves facing possible bankruptcy do have some property or income. Debt problems can happen to middle-income and even upper-income people. When that happens, paying the legal fees is not usually a serious problem.

If you are so badly off that you have no way to raise money for legal fees, it may be that you do not have that much to fear from creditors anyway—and therefore have less reason to file for bankruptcy. It may be that all of your property is exempt and cannot be taken from you (see Chapter 10), and your income is too small or of the wrong kind to be in danger of being garnished. There are precious few advantages to not having much property or income, but there is one—what you don't have, creditors can't take.

Sometimes family or friends will help with legal fees in order to free the petitioner from debt problems. You can also try to bargain with the lawyer; some will budge more easily and farther than others, but it is usually worth a shot.

When you have made the decision to file for bankruptcy or debt adjustment, you know that you will soon be coming under a court order that blocks creditors (see page 44). This may allow you to rethink your priorities about what debts most need to be paid—and where your lawyer's fees fit in.

Obviously, the fact that the bankruptcy is coming changes the consequences of dealing with creditors. Your lawyer should be able to advise you specifically on how to make decisions on whom and when to pay.

FINDING A BANKRUPTCY LAWYER

There is no foolproof way of finding a good bankruptcy lawyer—or, for that matter, a doctor or a carpenter. There are some methods, however, that may improve your chances.

The most obvious place to start looking is with a lawyer or law firm that has provided you with good service in the past. Not every law office handles bankruptcies, but they should all at least be able to recommend a lawyer who does.

Referrals

Next you should go to other people who can give you well-informed referrals. These might include a lawyer you know personally, someone who has been through a bankruptcy recently, or someone who is in business and deals with lawyers regularly. A referral may have two or more stages: You may get a referral to a good lawyer who does not handle bankruptcies but who can then recommend another who does.

But beware: Even a glowing recommendation is not a guarantee. Even a lawyer—much less a nonlawyer—may not be in a very good position to judge another lawyer's knowledge and ability. You are still the one responsible for making your own judgment about the person you are considering.

Advertising and Directories

Lawyers' advertising has become common in recent years, and consulting ads may work well for you. A healthy dose of caution and skepticism is needed, however. Most states have no formal system of specialization for lawyers, so a lawyer who advertises bankruptcy services isn't necessarily an expert.

There are some specialized directories that might help. The best is the *Law & Business Directory of Bankruptcy Attorneys.* [1] Larger public libraries may carry the book, and specialized law libraries will probably have it. This directory will tell you which lawyers in your area specialize in bankruptcy and whether they work mostly for debtors or creditors, for businesses or individuals.

---

[1] Prentice-Hall Law and Business.

Panel of Trustees

Though it may take some effort, this method is particularly helpful in finding a lawyer who is knowledgeable and up to date in bankruptcy law. A "trustee" is appointed by the court to review each bankruptcy case (see page 44). There is a list, or "panel," of people from which trustees are appointed for each federal court district or division. Many of those trustees are lawyers who also represent petitioners in other cases. Experience as a trustee is by no means a guarantee of excellence, but it does tell you that you are probably dealing with a lawyer who regularly works with bankruptcy law and knows his or her way around the local bankruptcy court.

Trustees also regularly get to see other lawyers representing their clients in bankruptcy court, and they review the legal documents those lawyers prepare. That makes trustees particularly well qualified to know which lawyers are good.

To get the list of trustees, find the Bankruptcy Court for your area. If you live in or near one of the larger cities in your state, look in the telephone book under "United States Government" for the "U.S. Trustee," probably under "Justice Department." If that doesn't work, call any U.S. Court or U.S. Justice Department number and ask how to reach the U.S. Trustee's office. If you don't know what city to look under for your Bankruptcy Court, your city or county court clerk may be able to refer you.

When you reach the right office, ask to be sent a list of the panel of private Chapter 7 trustees.

It is not common for anyone to ask for this list, so the clerk may be puzzled at first, but it is public information and you should be able to obtain it. There may be a copying charge. When you get the information, you will have an excellent list of possible lawyers or sources for referrals.

INTERVIEWING LAWYERS

The next and most important step in hiring a lawyer is to interview at least two of them. The best method of evaluating a lawyer is to sit down with him or her, discuss your situation, and then use your own best judgment, intelligence, and instincts. If you can compare two or more lawyers before you decide, your chances of choosing well will be greatly improved.

Meet with the lawyer in person as early as possible. Try to avoid doing too much of the initial conversation on the telephone, but bear in mind that the way lawyers proceed varies widely. Some lawyers send out general information on bankruptcy before the first meeting, but most do not. Thirty to forty-five minutes should be enough time for a first consultation in most consumer bankruptcy matters.

Try to see in person the lawyer who would be handling your case. Some lawyers have assistants do at least some of their screening or preliminary information gathering, and although there is nothing necessarily wrong with that, you should be wary if the lawyer seems too miserly with his or her time.

You should expect to spend a good part of the first meeting answering questions, as a lawyer obviously cannot advise you about your situation without understanding it thoroughly. But you should also be prepared to ask some questions.

Ask about the lawyer's experience. How many bankruptcy cases did he or she handle in the last year? If the answer is none or one, or if you don't get a straight answer, you have good reason to wonder how knowledgeable the attorney is. Numbers alone do not tell the whole story: A good general practitioner who does only a few bankruptcies a year may be very capable. But in general, the more recent experience a lawyer has with cases similar to yours, the better.

There are lawyers who are interested only in Chapter 7 and others who usually do only Chapter 13's. Steer clear of both kinds. Unless the lawyer handles both chapters and is open-minded about them, find someone else. You need balanced advice to help *you* make *your* decision.

Consider asking the lawyer for references from satisfied clients. This is not a common request, so the lawyer may be taken aback. Also, he or she will probably want time to get permission from clients to use their names. If you do talk to former clients, ask whether they were satisfied and what they did or did not like about the way the case was handled. Could they get through to the lawyer when they needed to? Is there anything they think you should watch out for?

Use information from former clients with caution. The lawyer is not going to steer you to an unhappy customer, and a client can't always tell when a lawyer is doing an excellent job or just an adequate one. But by encouraging the other person to talk, you may gain useful information.

Most of your questions to the lawyer will naturally be about your own situation. Asking questions and listening to the answers is the heart of the interview process.

After you have read this book carefully, you will be far better informed about bankruptcy than lawyers are used to seeing in their clients. This will be even more true as you talk to additional lawyers. My advice is not to hide your knowledge but not to wear it on your sleeve either. If the lawyer tells you something different from what you thought you knew, you might say, "I'm a little surprised to hear you say that. I had heard it was thus-and-so."

Then listen carefully to the answer. You will often find that the lawyer can back up what he or she has said, even when it seems to vary from what you have read. There are exceptions and variations to almost everything. Relatively slight differences in the facts of your situation, your state's laws, or even local court practices can make a big difference. Nevertheless, if the lawyer can't or won't back up his or her statements to your satisfaction, alarm bells should go off.

Don't be surprised if you get different advice from different lawyers. Even good bankruptcy lawyers may disagree. Dealing with debt problems is not a math exercise with one correct answer. All you can do is pin lawyers down as much as possible about the reasons for their advice, and then decide. It is your life and your money, and, when all is said and done, you are going to have to make the decisions.

Evaluate the advice you get, the effect it will have on your life, and your instinctive feelings about the lawyer. Does he or she seem honest and intelligent? Is he or she someone with whom you will be able to discuss your situation along the way?

DISCUSSING FEES

Before you go to the lawyer's office, you should know what, if any, fees you will be charged for the first appointment. You can also ask what the entire case will cost, but I suggest you not put too much emphasis on that. A lawyer may not be prepared to discuss fees until he or she knows more about the case. Try to choose the lawyers you will meet with on the basis of quality and worry about price later on.

Because fees vary greatly from time to time and place to place, only the most general guidelines can be offered here. An uncomplicated nonbusiness Chapter 7, however, should ordinarily cost between $500 and $1,000, and a Chapter 13 should be in that range or a little higher.

When you have reached the point where you are considering hiring a particular lawyer, you should discuss fees very specifically. Lawyers vary greatly in the fees they charge and how they go about figuring them. Many bankruptcy lawyers charge a flat fee that most often covers all of the services in a Chapter 7 or Chapter 13; others charge by the hour. Some require all of the fee in advance or at least before the petition is filed with the court; others will make different arrangements. In a Chapter 13, some lawyers will agree to take all or part of the legal fees through the court; under that arrangement, the lawyer gets payments out of what you put into the debt adjustment plan that is set up to pay your creditors.

Making sure that you get a fair deal on fees is another excellent reason for talking to more than one lawyer. The connection between price and quality in legal fees is not very strong. You can't assume that a premium price means premium service, and not all bargains are what they seem. But if you find more than one lawyer with whom you would be comfortable, you can certainly decide among them on the basis of cost.

DISCUSSING TIMING

Before you agree to hire a lawyer, get a clear and specific statement about how quickly the bankruptcy can be filed. Most lawyers are conscientious, but unfortunately, it is not unheard of for a client to pay the fee for a bankruptcy, provide the necessary information, and then wait indefinitely for the lawyer to act. If you have been careful in choosing a lawyer, the risk of that happening should be low, but you should have a clear understanding on this point and you should not be the least bit shy about holding the lawyer to his or her time commitments.

Preparing bankruptcy papers should rarely take more than a few weeks—even less in a simple case. Some law offices will prepare the papers on the spot the first time you go in. Unless you have a true legal emergency that can't wait a few days, I would advise you to refuse that procedure. It is much better to give yourself some time to think it over.

If you do need to file by a specific time for a reason such as a pending wage garnishment, be sure the lawyer knows that and agrees to do his or her part on time.

Even after you have talked to one or more lawyers, you do not necessarily have to rush into a decision. Unless you have a specific problem that forces you to act quickly, take as much time as you feel you need to make up your mind. Be wary of any lawyer who presses you to act quickly without good reason or who seems to be shading his or her advice to push you in that direction.

CHAPTER 5

BANKRUPTCY AND THE CHAPTER 13 ALTERNATIVE

People who petition for bankruptcy are as different as they could be in almost every way except one—they all have serious financial problems of one sort or another. The details of their situations vary widely. So do the approaches they take to the possibility of bankruptcy as a solution.

WHO IS ELIGIBLE FOR BANKRUPTCY?

If you think you might need to file for bankruptcy, being eligible is not likely to be a problem. You can get only one Chapter 7 discharge every six years, but there are few other restrictions.

A bankruptcy judge can refuse to issue a Chapter 7 discharge if granting it would be a "substantial abuse" of the law. It is not completely clear what that means, and judges have a good deal of individual choice. Some judges have said that anyone who has enough income to fund a Chapter 13 plan is not allowed to use Chapter 7. In practice, however, not many people actually seem to have been turned away from Chapter 7. The rule has generally been used only in extreme cases.

WHY PEOPLE *DON'T* FILE BANKRUPTCY

At any given time, there are millions of people who might theoretically be better off filing bankruptcy; they could discharge at least some of their debts and still protect their equity in property.

The majority of those people never consider bankruptcy because they feel their debts are under reasonable control. But even those who are in severe trouble may be reluctant. They see bankruptcy as an admission of failure. They fear the social stigma for themselves and their families. They worry that their reputations will be damaged. They may also worry about practical matters such as whether they'll ever get credit again. Some of these concerns, especially in smaller communities, are legitimate. Others are more psychological than real, but no less troublesome. Either kind can keep people from even exploring their legal rights.

THE ONE-TIME BAILOUT

For those who feel they have serious debt problems they can't handle any other way, bankruptcy may seem to be the only way out. It is, however, a method that can only be used once in many years, and you may want to save it until you have addressed the problems that got you into debt in the first place.

If you have so much debt, it may be hard to imagine how things could get even worse. There is at least one way: If you get a discharge of debts and a year or two later find yourself seriously in debt again, you will have all the same problems, with one important difference. You won't have the option of filing bankruptcy. After a bankruptcy discharge, you can't get another one in Chapter 7 for six years.

For this reason, if the problems that caused you to get

deeply into debt have not been taken care of, it may make sense to file a Chapter 13 repayment plan, rather than Chapter 7. But even that may not be a good idea until you are pretty sure that your finances are going to be under control.

No one expects you to able to foretell the future, and few people can be positive that they will not have new financial problems next week, next month, or next year. But until you are reasonably sure that your financial situation will be manageable, bankruptcy may be a serious mistake.

SHOULD YOU FILE BANKRUPTCY WHEN YOU HAVE NOTHING TO LOSE?

Having serious debt problems is not necessarily the same as what most people think of as being "broke." Some bankruptcy petitioners have good incomes and significant amounts of property, but they have debts that outweigh their resources.

Others have little property except household goods, and minimum-wage jobs or no job at all. If you are in that situation, there may be little point in bankruptcy because you have no assets or salary that need to be protected.

It may be that there is nothing creditors can do to you, even if they take you to court and win. Your wages can't be garnished until they reach a certain level. Income such as Social Security and public assistance cannot be garnished at all. Normal household goods are usually protected from creditors by the exemption laws. In any case, creditors rarely bother trying to seize them unless they have specific liens, and even then only as a last resort.

With limited income and assets, even if you have little or no hope of paying off your debts, there is something to be said for holding off on a bankruptcy filing. It may be better to wait for the time when you *do* have something to lose.

That means a good job with enough income to be in danger of wage garnishment, or some other financial improvement that gives you something to lose.

Making the decision to avoid or postpone bankruptcy, however, can be very uncomfortable because of pressures from bill collectors. For many people, the need to be free of the phone calls and late notices is so great that it outweighs other considerations.

It is entirely reasonable to consider those psychological factors in deciding whether to file for bankruptcy. But no one should file without thinking through the pros and cons, including the timing.

TAKING STEPS

Let's suppose you think you might need to file bankruptcy or Chapter 13 and have chosen a particular lawyer to discuss it with.

The lawyer first needs to know your overall financial situation, even if your problems seem to focus on a few problem debts. The lawyer or an assistant gets this information from conversation, written questionnaires, or a combination of the two.

The lawyer also should understand how you feel about your situation and what your objectives are. Until you have decided where you want to go, a lawyer can't help you get there, and you should use your first meeting to explore your goals with your attorney.

A good bankruptcy lawyer should be able to tell you what your basic options are after a meeting of half an hour to an hour. When you have provided the detailed information needed for the papers, the lawyer puts them in final form for your signature. The signed papers can then be filed with the court, and the case will proceed as we will see in Chapter 6.

THE CHAPTER 13 ALTERNATIVE

Even if you ask only about bankruptcy, which requires no payments on most debts, lawyers are specifically required by law to tell you about debt repayment plans, or Chapter 13.

Most people who ask for protection under the Bankruptcy Code choose Chapter 7. Those who choose Chapter 13 fall into two general groups: Some are seeking certain specific legal or financial advantages; others just want to make partial payments on their debts, instead of asking for a total discharge.

THE LEGAL BENEFITS OF CHAPTER 13

If you are in any of the following situations, you may be legally or financially better off with Chapter 13, instead of Chapter 7:

A Previous Bankruptcy Within Six Years   If you have already filed for bankruptcy and received a discharge of debts, you cannot get another one in Chapter 7 for six years. However, you can still file under Chapter 13.

When someone makes repeated bankruptcy filings of any kind, however, something is obviously wrong. There is something about that person's life or finances that no type of bankruptcy will fix. Courts tend to take a much closer look at petitioners who keep coming back with new cases.

A "Substantial Abuse" Ruling   A person who has been turned away from Chapter 7 under this rarely used rule (see page 33) can usually file under Chapter 13.

Nondischargeable Debts   Some kinds of debts that would not be eliminated by a Chapter 7 discharge (see page 47) can at least be reduced in a Chapter 13. One example is a debt based on fraud. By making partial payments over three years, the debtor can sometimes resolve a debt that would not be discharged by a Chapter 7.

Mortgage Default   Chapter 13 has rules allowing the petitioner to "cure a default" on a long-term contract. This procedure is most often used to restore home mortgages to good standing.

This rule may be useful if you have fallen behind in your mortgage payments and are willing and able to catch up on them but the bank or mortgage company will not cooperate. A Chapter 13 plan can require the mortgage company to accept catch-up payments and return the mortgage to good standing.

This procedure will not help if you have fallen behind because you don't have enough income to swing the mortgage payments. It will work only if you are going to be able to stay current in the future. Otherwise, finding a cheaper place to live may be the only answer.

Protecting a Cosigner   Cosigners are usually friends or relatives. People with debt problems are often very concerned with protecting people who have cosigned for them.

If you are in that situation, a Chapter 7 may not help. The creditor can still collect from your cosigner even if the bankruptcy discharge protects you. You may be able to take care of the problem simply by continuing to make payments on the cosigned debt after the Chapter 7. Even though only your cosigner still has a legal obligation to pay, creditors usually don't care whose money they are getting.

If that isn't good enough, a Chapter 13 may be the answer because it usually prevents the creditor from taking any collection action against a cosigner if the plan pays the debt in full.

Nonexempt Property   If you have property that would not be exempt and would be taken by the trustee in a Chapter 7, you may be able to keep it by filing a Chapter 13 instead. In order for this to work, your Chapter 13 payments must be large enough that all creditors receive as much money as they would have if the property had been sold in a Chapter 7.

Need to Force a Reaffirmation Chapter 7 petitioners can often make "reaffirmation agreements" (see page 76) and keep property on which a creditor still has a lien. Paying off the debt under a Chapter 13 can work out to about the same thing.

The secured portion of the debt—that is, the part backed up by dollar value in collateral—must be paid in full in a Chapter 13, or the collateral must be surrendered. But under this plan, the creditor often has no choice about accepting stretched-out payments.

A Chapter 13 can be useful if you are worried that you will not be able to reach agreement with a creditor to retain an important piece of property that you've pledged as collateral. If you have several such situations, consolidating the payments in a Chapter 13 plan may be a good method.

Need for Flexibility Once a Chapter 7 petition is filed, it is very difficult to withdraw it. It is not a good idea to file one unless you are committed to going through with the entire process.

A Chapter 13 petition, on the other hand, can be withdrawn at any time before or after a plan is confirmed. If you need protection from creditors but are not ready to be locked in to all of the provisions of the bankruptcy law, you may prefer Chapter 13.

A petitioner may need the protection of the bankruptcy law but not be sure that the source of the debt problems has been resolved—for example, there may be a continuing accumulation of medical bills. Under those circumstances, a Chapter 13 offers protection from creditors without using up the once-in-six-years right to seek a Chapter 7 discharge.

A Chapter 13 petitioner can switch to Chapter 7 at any time, and a Chapter 7 can be converted to Chapter 13 in the same way; the law allows one free switch. Any changes after that require the permission of the judge. In practice, far more Chapter 13's are converted to Chapter 7's than the other way around.

Better Credit   Some petitioners believe—or hope—that making Chapter 13 payments instead of filing Chapter 7 will pay off in a better credit rating later on. This reasoning is pretty shaky, as we will see in Chapter 12.

THE UNFORCED CHAPTER 13

All Chapter 13's are voluntary in the sense that creditors cannot legally force a debtor into this procedure, as they technically can with a Chapter 7. But some Chapter 13's are filed not for legal advantages but because petitioners want to pay as much of their debts as possible, even though they cannot meet the original payments or pay the full amounts of the debts. This is a choice a petitioner must make for him- or herself. A lawyer can explain what is possible, but beyond that it really doesn't matter what the lawyer thinks about this particular decision.

THE DISADVANTAGES OF CHAPTER 13

Chapter 7's are filed more than twice as often as Chapter 13, and only about a quarter of those Chapter 13's are approved and completed. There are good reasons why Chapter 7 predominates:

• Chapter 13 requires a three-year payment plan, while Chapter 7 does not.

- Chapter 13's tend to be more expensive. The Chapter 13 trustee receives a commission on all payments processed through his or her office.
- Chapter 13's are slightly more complicated legally and lawyers' fees tend to be a little higher.
- Not everyone is eligible for Chapter 13. To qualify, your regular income must be large enough to make the plan workable. You may not have more than $250,000 in unsecured debts and $750,000 in secured debts.

If you need to file a bankruptcy petition of some kind but have more debts than are allowed in Chapter 13, you still have some choices. In addition to Chapter 7, you may be eligible for Chapter 11, the more complicated and expensive debt reorganization designed primarily for businesses. Family farmers may be eligible for Chapter 12, a modified version of Chapter 13.

SETTING UP A CHAPTER 13 PLAN

If you file a Chapter 13, you must work out a specific debt repayment plan and submit it to the court. The court doesn't directly tell you what you must pay. You offer a plan and the court says yes or no. For example, one plan may say that the petitioner will pay $200 per month for three years. Another may require the petitioner to pay $300 per month until all debts are paid in full.

There are several things that have to be considered in putting together a Chapter 13 plan:

Ability to Pay You must file a budget showing that you have enough income to pay all your current expenses and still make the Chapter 13 payment. Even if the law didn't require this, common sense would. There is no point in going to the trouble and expense of setting up a Chapter 13 if the payments aren't workable. The budget may be questioned by creditors or the trustee if it appears either excessively high or unrealistically low.

Specific Objectives That Must Be Met   If you have chosen Chapter 13 to for a specific legal reason, you must make payments large enough to reach that goal. For instance, if you want to prevent a creditor from going after a cosigner, the Chapter 13 payments must be large enough to pay the debt in full. If the goal is to keep collateral—a car, for example—its value must be paid in full to clear the lien.

Repayment plans can do very little picking and choosing among creditors, so if you pay a certain amount to one creditor, you may have to pay the same percentage to others.

Structure of Payments   The most common pattern for Chapter 13 payments is a certain amount per month for three years, but many variations are possible:

- Plans can run for as long as five years. This is useful if you need to pay a certain amount to achieve a particular objective but cannot make large enough payments to do it in three years.
- For petitioners with seasonal income or other variations from a regular paycheck, payments don't necessarily have to be in a set monthly amount.
- A plan can provide for increasing your payments over the term if there is reason to expect that your income will increase to cover them. Such "graduated payment" plans may receive a closer review than others, however, because they can be unfair to creditors. A petitioner can try to buy time with such a plan by promising eventually to make a large total of payments without having to deliver in the short run.

CHAPTER 6

THE BANKRUPTCY PROCESS

In this section we will take a look at what happens in a Chapter 7 bankruptcy and then in a Chapter 13 debt adjustment so that we can later examine the key areas of bankruptcy law and procedure, including debts, property, liens on property, and exempt property.

THE LEGAL PROCESS FOR A CHAPTER 7 BANKRUPTCY

As we have seen, though it is possible to file for bankruptcy without a lawyer, most people do hire one. The following steps will be taken by a lawyer or an individual in the proceeding.

Filing the Bankruptcy Petition

A Chapter 7 bankruptcy case begins with the filing of a set of papers at the office of the bankruptcy court. "Filing" simply means sending or taking the papers to the court office.

Those papers include detailed lists—called "schedules"—showing the property owned by the petitioner, the creditors to whom the money is owed, and some other financial and background information. These papers are attached to a formal request for bankruptcy, the "petition" itself.

A married couple can file a single case as joint petitioners.

In this book, the word "petitioner" usually applies to both a husband and wife when they are filing for bankruptcy together.

The Automatic Stay

As soon as the clerk in the bankruptcy court office receives the papers and stamps them as filed, a sweeping federal court order goes into effect. That order forbids nearly all debt collection activity by creditors against that petitioner. Collection letters, telephone calls, and routine bills are ordered stopped. Even lawsuits in other courts have to be suspended.

This court order is usually known as the "automatic stay." In legal terminology, a "stay" is an order that something *not* be done. The stay stops some creditors permanently—those whose claims are eventually going to be discharged. The automatic stay gives most petitioners the key benefit of the bankruptcy—protection from creditors—immediately.

Some creditors' actions may be stopped only temporarily by the stay and then resumed later. One common example of that might be a mortgage foreclosure. (See Chapter 7 for debts that survive bankruptcy.)

Within a couple of weeks after the papers are filed, the court sends out a notice to all creditors, telling them that the bankruptcy has been started and the stay is in effect. The petitioner's lawyer can notify some creditors even sooner, if that is necessary to stop a lawsuit or wage garnishment.

The Bankruptcy Trustee

As soon as a bankruptcy case is filed a trustee is assigned to protect the interests of the creditors. He or she determines if the petitioner has any property that legally can and should be sold so that the proceeds can be applied to the listed debts. The trustee is usually a lawyer and is chosen from a list or panel of trustees for each court district.

The trustee may also review the petitioner's recent financial history, including payments made to creditors shortly before filing and certain other transactions. In that way the trustee can sometimes regain property transferred by the petitioner and redistribute its value among the creditors.

For example, if you paid your brother $1,000 that you owe him shortly before filing bankruptcy or transferred an item of property to him, the trustee may get the money or property back. The money may then be paid to creditors "higher on the list" than your brother, or possibly shared evenly among him and other creditors.

The trustee has authority to investigate, but the common fear that bankruptcy will lead to a search or inventory of the petitioner's home has almost no basis. It very rarely happens. A judge would not authorize such action without strong reason to believe that the petitioner has valuable items that have not been declared and that might qualify for being sold by the trustee.

The Hearing

The petitioner must attend a court hearing about a month after the petition is filed. This hearing is officially called a "meeting of creditors," but often no creditors actually attend.

Basically the hearing is an informational session, much like what is called a "deposition" in other kinds of court cases. The trustee and any creditors who choose to take part can ask the petitioner to testify under oath that the information in the papers is accurate, and to answer other questions about his or her financial situation.

The trustee runs the hearing. The bankruptcy judge does not attend, and many petitioners never even see the judge. The meeting of creditors is often the only court hearing in a routine case. It is less formal than many court proceedings and may be held in a conference room or office rather than an actual courtroom.

There may be some discussion at the hearing about a

"statement of intention" or "complying with Section 341." This has to do with a law requiring the petitioner to discuss with creditors how accounts with liens will be handled. The possibilities include surrendering the collateral to the creditor and "reaffirming" the debt, or agreeing to keep paying it (see page 76). Exactly how this process is handled varies considerably from one state to another.

Many bankruptcies are pretty much over after the meeting of creditors. In routine cases, all that is left is to wait about two months for certain time limits to expire, so the court can issue the final discharge-of-debts order. There is sometimes a brief second court hearing to approve any reaffirmation agreements that the petitioner has reached with creditors.

After the Hearing

Some bankruptcies are not that simple. In the weeks after the hearing, several types of complications can arise.

Claims on Property   The trustee may decide that some of the petitioner's property should be sold and the proceeds applied to the debts. The petitioner can challenge such a claim on property before the judge if there is a legal dispute about the trustee's rights.

Dischargeability Cases   Any creditor may file a lawsuit in the bankruptcy court contesting the bankruptcy. Creditors may claim either that the particular debts owed to them by the petitioner should not be discharged or that the petitioner is not entitled to discharge any debts at all. All objections of either kind must be cleared up before the overall bankruptcy case can be closed.

Reaffirmation Agreement   After the hearing, the petitioner may reaffirm some debts and agree to continue paying those creditors. The usual reason for a reaffirmation is to keep some property on which the creditor still has a lien and that might otherwise be repossessed. (For information on liens, see Chapter 9).

Reaffirmations are specifically regulated to protect petitioners from being pressured into signing away the benefits of bankruptcy. Either court approval or a lawyer's signature is required on a reaffirmation agreement, and the petitioner has sixty days to cancel the agreement.

Discharge of Debts

The point of filing a Chapter 7 is usually to receive the court order that discharges debts. The discharge permanently forbids creditors from trying to collect those debts to which it applies. By the discharge order, the temporary protection of the stay order is put into place forever as far as those particular debts are concerned.

Creditors may not file lawsuits or start wage garnishment proceedings on discharged debts. They may not send collection letters or make telephone calls. Any act a creditor might take to collect such debts violates the discharge.

The discharge also stops some unusual and indirect kinds of debt collection:

- In some states, a driver who gets into an accident without insurance can have his or her license and registration suspended until any damage claims are paid. The discharge overrides those laws and allows the petitioner to get the license back.
- Colleges sometimes refuse to issue transcripts of grades until tuition bills or student loans are paid. If the debt is discharged, they cannot do that. (As we will see, however, student loans are harder to discharge than most debts.)
- Employers cannot discriminate against someone solely because of a bankruptcy, nor, in most situations, can the government.

After the Discharge of Debts Is Granted

The court usually issues the discharge a few months after the case is filed, and most bankruptcy cases can then be closed. After that, most petitioners are more or less home free and can forget about the bankruptcy and the discharged debts.

But not always: In a few cases, problems come up months or years later. Some creditors may claim that the debts owed to them were not covered by the discharge. Or creditors may try to collect an old debt because either a misunderstanding or poor record keeping has kept the debt from being taken off their books.

In either case, the petitioner must be prepared to protect his or her rights. Even if a lawsuit or wage garnishment violates the discharge, the petitioner may have to go back into court to stop it. The court personnel where the lawsuit or garnishment is filed probably won't know about the bankruptcy until the petitioner points it out.

THE LEGAL PROCESS FOR A CHAPTER 13 DEBT ADJUSTMENT

The early stages of a Chapter 13 debt adjustment case are much the same as those of a Chapter 7. A similar set of papers is filed, the same stay order against creditors goes into effect, a trustee is appointed, and a "meeting of creditors" hearing is held.

In a Chapter 13, however, the petitioner prepares a plan for repayment of debts and files it along with the original papers or soon afterward. This plan sets out the petitioner's proposal for making debt payments over a period of time—up to five years, but usually three.

Some types of debts have to be paid in full during the Chapter 13 for the court to approve the plan. Other debts can be reduced and only partially paid. The trustee and creditors can object to the plan if they believe it does not conform to the legal requirements.

If someone does object to the plan, the judge holds a separate hearing to determine if the plan will be approved, or "confirmed." If no one objects, the judge must still review the plan but can confirm it without holding a hearing.

If the judge does turn down the plan, the petitioner has three choices:

- Adjust the plan to rectify the problems that caused it to be rejected and then ask again for confirmation
- Drop the Chapter 13 case
- Switch to a Chapter 7 case and ask for a discharge of debts without offering a repayment plan

When the judge has approved the plan, the payments are sent to the trustee. Payments are often made by deductions from the petitioner's paycheck. The trustee then pays the money to creditors according to formulas set by the law and by the confirmed plan.

The Chapter 13 payments cover only past debts. The petitioner continues to pay most current expenses directly. These include such things as utilities, medical expenses or insurance, other insurance, food and clothing, and car repairs.

If the Chapter 13 payments are not made on time, the case can be dismissed. Also, either the petitioner or a creditor can ask the court to modify the plan to deal with changed circumstances.

When all payments provided for by the plan are completed, any remaining debts are discharged and the case is closed.

CHAPTER 7

DEBTS

A debt can be a simple thing: I owe you so much money with no conditions, no collateral, and no dispute about the amount.

But debts also come with as many variations and complications as people can think up, and bankruptcy law has to deal with all of them.

A debt can be owed to almost anyone—a bank, credit card company, public utility, friend, relative, doctor, landlord, even the government. And those are only examples. Whenever you owe money for any reason or when anyone even *thinks* you owe them money, for bankruptcy purposes there is a debt.

We will look first at some of the major kinds of debts, and then at what happens to them in bankruptcy.

SECURED AND UNSECURED DEBTS

A debt is "secured" if it is backed up by a lien on any kind of property owned by the debtor. A "lien" is a creditor's special right to take and sell a particular item of property, if necessary, to pay the debt. (See Chapter 9 for more information on liens.)

Two of the most common examples of secured debts are home mortgages and purchase loans on cars. A secured debt, however, can be supported by a lien on almost any type of property.

At the time their sporting goods business fails, Dave and Beth Wilson own a house worth $150,000 and owe $130,000 on a mortgage secured by it.

Thomas Martinez, the construction worker, owns a car worth $5,000 but owes $7,000 on the car loan he took out to buy it. The car secures the car loan.

An unsecured debt is not backed by collateral. Generally speaking, an "unsecured creditor" has far fewer rights in bankruptcy and usually can't stop the debt from being completely discharged.

Susan Novak has no property that is pledged as collateral. All of her debts, including her student loans and medical bills, are unsecured.

OTHER TYPES OF DEBTS

Though "secured" and "unsecured" are the only classifications required for most bankruptcy cases, other variations are referred to on the official bankruptcy forms:

Disputed Debts

A disputed debt is one that is denied or at least partially contested by the person who is supposed to owe it. Bankruptcy is designed to deal with the petitioner's whole financial situation. To do that, even a contested debt claim must be taken into account.

Susan Novak is being billed for some medical services she says were included in a bill she already paid. Although she disputes that bill, she cannot risk forgetting about it as long as the hospital is still trying to collect it from her. She would need to list it if she filed bankruptcy papers.

If it becomes necessary to decide whether the debt is really owed and in what amount, the bankruptcy judge can either make that decision or allow the parties to take the case to another court. It usually doesn't matter in a Chapter 7 because the debt is eliminated either way. In a Chapter 13, where debts are at least partially paid, it may be important.

Matured and Unmatured Debts

An unmatured debt is one that isn't due yet. If I borrowed money and agreed to pay it back at a specific time that hasn't arrived yet, that debt is unmatured. Although I owe the money, I don't have to pay it yet.

> The Wilsons received one loan that was to be repaid with interest in a single payment after two years. When their sports business closed, they still had six months to go. That loan is an unmatured debt.

The most common kind of unmatured debt is the installment contract. As long as the borrower makes the payments on time, the debt for the future installments is unmatured. The money is owed, but the creditor has no legal right to force payment until the due date.

The borrower can, however, easily lose the right to pay in installments if he or she misses payments. If that happens, the creditor can "accelerate" the loan, making the full amount due immediately.

An unmatured debt can still be a major problem when the person who owes it realizes that he or she will not be able to pay when it becomes due.

Contingent Debts

A debt is "contingent" if the debtor is required to pay only if certain things happen in the future, and it is not clear when or if they will happen. Even the courts have trouble explaining it any more clearly than that.

The most common kind of contingent debt comes from

cosigning or guaranteeing a debt owed by someone else. In other words, only if that person fails to pay at the specified time do you become responsible for the debt.

Unliquidated Debts

The word *liquidated* here means "fixed to a specific or easily calculated dollar amount," as most debts are.

An unliquidated debt may, for example, come from an accident situation where someone has accidentally injured you and admits owing you damages for the injury. Until the amount is set by either a lawsuit or a negotiation, the debt for the injury damages is unliquidated.

"Combination" Debts

A single debt can sometimes fall into more than one category. If, in the example we've just seen, responsibility for the accident is not yet resolved, the debt has two of these elements—as in a situation the Wilsons faced:

> A customer of D&B Sports Center who fell in the store and got hurt has claimed it was the owners' fault. He wants $10,000 from Dave and Beth. They don't think they owe a cent, but they still have to protect themselves from the claim. They owe an unliquidated, disputed debt to the customer. They would have to list the customer as a creditor in a bankruptcy.

Cosigned Debts

When one person cosigns or guarantees a debt for someone else, the debt relationships get complicated:

> One of Susan Novak's early student loans was cosigned by her mother. Susan still owes that debt to the student loan agency, just as she would any other. Her mother owes a contingent debt to the lender; she will have to pay if Susan doesn't. If Mrs. Novak does end up having to pay it off, she may have a legal right to try to get her money back from Susan. (Like most mothers, she probably wouldn't do that, but she could.) Even the *possibility* that this might eventually happen means that *Susan* owes a contingent debt to her *mother.*

A Chapter 7 bankruptcy protects the person who actually files, but not a cosigner. If you file, the creditor can still try to collect from your cosigner.

COMPILING THE LIST OF DEBTS FOR FILING BANKRUPTCY

The Bankruptcy Code defines "debt" very broadly. All the categories we have just looked at and more are covered. A petitioner's debt list should include not only anyone to whom he or she owes money, or might owe money, but everyone who might think they are owed something.

The law requires a complete list, and it is very much to the petitioner's advantage to see that every possible creditor gets notice of the bankruptcy and is clearly covered by it. If a debt is inadvertently omitted from the list, it may be discharged anyway, but that depends on the circumstances. A petitioner is much better off being very thorough with the list and not having to worry about unlisted debts.

WHAT DEBTS ARE NOT DISCHARGED

Putting a debt on the list filed with the court does not guarantee that it will be discharged. There are several groups of debts that are not eliminated by a bankruptcy (though some of them can be managed in a Chapter 13 debt adjustment):

Secured Debts
Secured debts are those backed by collateral. Because the creditor holds a lien on property, discharging the debt often doesn't do the petitioner much good. To keep the collateral—a house, a car, an appliance—the petitioner may still

have to pay the creditor. (See Chapter 9 for what happens to secured debts in bankruptcy.)

Other debts that are not eliminated by bankruptcy are those the law gives special protection from being discharged. The following categories are included:

Taxes

It is no news to most people that taxes are usually not discharged in bankruptcy. Even people who know something about the subject are often surprised to learn that *some* taxes *can* be discharged.

The rules are complicated. For an income tax debt to qualify for discharge, it must be at least three years old. The tax return involved must have been made truthfully. Other rules involve the amount of time that has passed since the taxes were officially assessed. However, even if those discharge rules are met, a tax lien may prevent the petitioner from effectively getting free of the debt.

Bankruptcy law is even tougher on some kinds of business taxes. Sales taxes or payroll withholding taxes that were not paid to the government are not discharged, no matter how old they are.

> When times got tough at their store, the Wilsons fell behind on both sales tax and payroll deduction payments to the state and federal governments. They still owe that money, and a Chapter 7 bankruptcy will not eliminate those debts.

If taxes are not discharged, they are "priority claims" in the bankruptcy. That means that if the trustee collects some money from the petitioner's property, it goes to pay taxes ahead of most other creditors. In many bankruptcies, of course, there is no money to pay *any* creditor, so it doesn't matter who would have come first. But when money is available, taxes usually get the first shot at it.

In most states, real estate taxes are liens on the property to which they apply, even ahead of mortgages, so they are not eliminated by bankruptcy. Property taxes usually stay with the property, and whoever ends up with the property has to pay them to get a clear title.

There is no blanket rule that keeps all debts owed to the government from being discharged. There is special protection for taxes and several other specific categories of debts that are always or often owed to the government, including fines and student loans. But if a debt to a government agency doesn't fall into one of those specific categories, it can be discharged like any other.

Luxury Goods

A debt for more than $1,000 of luxury goods or services bought within sixty days before bankruptcy may be nondischargeable. Luxury goods are those not reasonably needed to support or maintain the petitioner's family.

Alimony and Child Support

Court-ordered payments for support of the petitioner's children, spouse, or former spouse are not dischargeable.

Payments ordered by the court in a divorce, however, are not always support or alimony. Divorce courts sometimes order payments to balance out the division of property. Such a property division debt may or may not be dischargeable. The court must weigh whether the petitioner has sufficient income or resources to pay it after the bankruptcy. The court must also compare the relative damage to the petitioner and the ex-spouse from discharging or not discharging a property settlement debt.

It is not always clear whether particular divorce-related debt is support or property settlement. The way the payment is described in the divorce papers does not always determine what will happen in bankruptcy court. Bankruptcy judges frequently must decide which kind of payment the court is dealing with in a particular case in order to determine which discharge rules apply.

Student Loans

The rules on discharging a student loan are almost as complicated as the ones covering taxes.

Generally, a student loan is not dischargeable in a Chapter 7 case until seven years after repayment on it was supposed to start. Under many loan programs, payments begin six or nine months after the student was last in school at least half time. Therefore, it takes nearly eight years from when the student leaves school for student loans to become dischargeable.

More recent student loans are not discharged in a Chapter 7. The seven-year period is figured to the day the bankruptcy is filed. If the student has received any deferments of payment—for military service or teaching, for example—those periods are added to the seven years. Obviously, that makes the calculations even more difficult. The same is true if the student has been in and out of school since the loan was taken out. Signing a refinancing or consolidation agreement can restart the seven years.

All of Susan Novak's student loans were within the seven-year period and would not be discharged in a Chapter 7.

Beth Wilson also had some small amounts left on student loans. Since she had been out of school for more than nine years, her loans would be dischargeable.

Under many student loan programs, the debt is forgiven if the student dies, and it *may* be discharged even before the seven years are up if repaying it would be an "undue hardship" for the petitioner or his or her dependents. Very few petitioners qualify under this exception. Courts generally rule that repaying student loans is a hardship for anyone, and unusually severe circumstances are needed to make an "undue" hardship.

Even stricter rules apply to loans granted to students in medical school, nursing, or related fields under the Health Education Assistance Loan (HEAL) program. There is no hardship rule at all, and even after seven years some additional restrictions apply.

Drunken Driving Damages

Debts for physical injuries or death caused by the petitioner while driving while legally intoxicated or impaired by drugs may not be discharged. This rule does apply to property damage claims, which are dischargeable.

False Financial Statement

If the creditor can show that the petitioner got credit by using a false written statement about his or her financial condition, the debt may not be discharged. Most commonly, the creditor will claim that this false or incomplete information appeared on an application for a loan or other credit. Failure to list all previous debts is one of the most common complaints.

It is not enough that the information be false or even deliberately false. The creditor must show that he or she really was misled by the wrong information and made a loan or gave credit that wouldn't have been granted otherwise.

Fraud or False Pretenses

The discharge may not cover a debt resulting from fraud. Credit card charges run up on a closed account may come under this category.

Embezzlement, Larceny, Malicious Injury, and Fines

Debts resulting from criminal activity generally are not dischargeable. In addition, although the law itself doesn't clearly say so, courts have ruled that a court order for restitution to a crime victim is legally a form of fine and therefore not dischargeable.

When a debtor has sold collateral on which a creditor holds a lien, it may be considered "malicious injury." The petitioner may still have to pay at least the value of the collateral the creditor should have received.

Unscheduled Debts

If a creditor is not listed on the forms filed with the court, the creditor doesn't get the official notice of the bankruptcy and therefore *may* not be covered by the discharge.

In fact, unlisted debts are often discharged anyway. This is likely to be true if the petitioner has acted in good faith and has not tried to deceive anyone and no money was paid to the creditors who did get notice.

HOW IT IS DECIDED WHETHER A DEBT IS DISCHARGEABLE

It is up to the creditor to show the bankruptcy court that a debt should not be discharged. In some cases, if the creditor doesn't do so promptly, the debt is discharged. This rule applies to the following categories:
- False financial statement
- Fraud or false pretenses
- Purchase of luxury goods
- Malicious injury
- Divorce property settlement

A creditor that believes a debt fits into one of these categories must make that claim to the bankruptcy court within sixty days after the "meeting of creditors" hearing.

A more flexible rule applies when a creditor claims its debt survives under one of the other categories, including taxes, alimony, student loans, and drunken driving. The creditor does not lose any rights in these kinds of debts, even by ignoring the Chapter 7 case. If there is a dispute as to whether a debt falls into one of those categories, it may be brought up in another court when the creditor tries to collect the debt. Bankruptcy cases may also be reopened to decide this type of dispute months or even years after they have been completed.

These rules work in such a way that most petitioners can feel safe once they have the discharge; they aren't very likely to be surprised later about a debt that has survived the bankruptcy. The kinds of objections that most often come as a surprise tend to be ones that are covered by the sixty-day rule.

THE CREDITOR'S DILEMMA

When a debt might be protected from discharge for one of the reasons to which the sixty-day rule applies, a creditor often has a tough choice to make. If the creditor does not object on time, those rights are lost and the debt is discharged like any other. But to file objections, creditors must pay both a stiff filing fee and their own lawyer's fees. If they lose, they may have to pay the petitioner's legal fees as well.

Even a creditor that succeeds gains only the right to keep trying to collect the debt, usually from someone who does not have much money anyway. The smaller the debt, the harder it is to justify the expense of fighting over it.

As a result, many debts that might legally be eligible to survive the bankruptcy are discharged anyway, without an objection ever being filed.

When Thomas Martinez filed a Chapter 7, he had several debts on which he was concerned that he might run into a "false financial statement" problem. He had not always been completely thorough in listing his other debts on loan applications.

His lawyer told him that worrying about it wouldn't help; they would just have to wait and see what happened. In fact, only one creditor filed an objection. Thomas's lawyer made it clear that they were prepared to contest in court whether the creditor had really been misled by any wrong information. The creditor accepted a settlement of payments totaling about a third of the debt.

COMPLETE DENIAL OF DISCHARGE

If a creditor or the trustee can prove the petitioner committed certain kinds of misconduct, the judge may deny him or her a discharge of *any* debts.

The kinds of misconduct required include destruction or unexplained loss of property, destruction of records, and failing to follow court orders. Total denial of discharge is rare and most often involves people who have been in business.

When a discharge is denied in a personal case, the reason is usually failure to show up for court dates or ignoring court orders.

VOLUNTARY REPAYMENTS

A petitioner can pay off a debt voluntarily even after it has been discharged in bankruptcy. Nothing about a bankruptcy prevents you from later paying off whatever debts you wish to. No written agreement is needed to do that.

A petitioner may sign a formal, legally binding agreement to keep paying a discharged debt only when there is some specific legal or financial advantage. Usually that reason is to keep collateral that otherwise could be repossessed.

Even when a petitioner intends all along to pay a particular debt, it still has to be listed on the official papers. The petitioner must swear under oath that the list includes all creditors, not just those that he or she wants to discharge.

CHAPTER 8

PROPERTY

The broad net that sweeps all kinds of debts into bankruptcy is matched by one that takes in just as wide a range of property. What happens to those kinds of property in bankruptcy? Working out the answers is even more complicated than answering the same questions about debts.

WHAT "PROPERTY" INCLUDES

A list of examples is the best way to get a sense of how broad the concept of property in bankruptcy is—although even these examples by no means cover everything.
  Property includes:
- Real estate (land or buildings)
- Cars and other vehicles
- Furniture, appliances, and other household goods
- Stocks and bonds
- Cash
- Clothing and jewelry
- Accounts with banks, savings and loans, and credit unions
- Rights to money that is owed to the petitioner by others
- Money of the petitioner that is being held as a security deposit
- Tax refunds due to be received by the petitioner
- Inheritances

- Businesses or business equipment and inventory
- Antiques or other collections
- Works of art
- Sporting goods
- Firearms
- Life insurance
- Retirement or pension accounts

To put it another way, property is pretty much everything a petitioner owns or has financial rights in. Bankruptcy may also affect property the petitioner is only renting or leasing.

As with debts, all property owned by a petitioner must be listed in the papers filed with the court. What happens to the property in bankruptcy is an entirely different question.

TRUST FUNDS

One of the very few kinds of property that bankruptcy doesn't reach are certain trust funds under which heirs or other beneficiaries receive payments over a period of time.

When a trust fund is set up with what is called a "spendthrift clause," creditors are barred from getting at those payments. The people who are getting the money can collect the payments even if they owe money and have court judgments against them. Even a beneficiary who goes through Chapter 7 can keep the rights to those payments.

Beth Wilson's grandmother left her some money in a trust account from which Beth receives about $1,000 a year in interest. Even though the trust payments are as good as money in the bank for many purposes, creditors would not be able to get at them because of the restrictions in the trust papers. Even if Beth files for bankruptcy, this money is still protected.

This rule does not apply when the petitioner set up the trust fund for him- or herself. Trust payments are protected only when the petitioner is receiving benefits from a fund established by someone else.

Most pension plans are kept out of the employee's bankruptcy by this rule as well.

PROPERTY ACQUIRED AFTER FILING BANKRUPTCY

Property, including earned wages, that the petitioner obtains *after* filing a Chapter 7 bankruptcy is usually not affected by or involved in the bankruptcy. The debts and property covered by a Chapter 7 are essentially locked in at the date of filing.

But there are some exceptions to this rule, too: Even after a bankruptcy filing, inheritances and divorce property settlements are included in the bankruptcy if less than six months have passed since the petitioner became eligible to receive them.

A paycheck in process when the bankruptcy is filed—one earned before filing but due to be paid after filing—is technically property in the bankruptcy. Legally, it is a debt owed to the petitioner by his or her employer when the bankruptcy is filed.

At least part of the check might be protected as exempt property anyway; state law and court decisions disagree on that point. Even if it is not, however, that technicality is ignored in some localities and the petitioner is allowed to treat it like any other paycheck and keep the money.

WHAT HAPPENS TO PROPERTY IN BANKRUPTCY

Chapter 7 bankruptcy affects each item of the petitioner's property in one of three general ways:

Property Encumbered by a Lien   If property is tied up by a lien and bankruptcy does not remove that lien, the petitioner and that creditor stay in much the same relationship as they were. They must sort out the rights to the property between themselves either during or after the bankruptcy.

> The Wilsons owned a car they could have sold for $11,000. The balance on the loan on it was almost $12,000. Since the entire value of the car was tied up, a bankruptcy trustee would have no interest in it. If the car were sold, all the money would go to pay the car loan anyway, and there would be nothing left for other creditors.

Exempt Property   The law allows a petitioner to keep certain types of property free from all claims of creditors except those who have specific liens (see Chapter 10).

> Susan Novak had an older used car worth about $800. There was no lien on the car, but the exempt property laws allowed her to keep a car with a value of up to $1,200. If she filed bankruptcy, she could keep the car as exempt.

Nonexempt Property   If there is property that is neither tied up by liens nor exempt, the trustee can take control of it and sell it. The proceeds are used to pay the petitioner's debts.

A single item of property may be split between two or more categories. If only part of the value of an item is tied up by a lien, the remaining value or "equity" may either be available to be taken by the trustee or protected as exempt.

> Dave and Beth Wilson owned a second car worth $12,000. They owed $8,000 on that car loan, so they had $4,000 of equity. The exemption laws allowed them to protect $1,000 of that. In a Chapter 7 bankruptcy the trustee might sell the car for the $12,000. He or she could then use $8,000 to pay off the loan, pay the Wilsons $1,000 as their exemption, and use the remaining $3,000 to pay their other creditors.

THE BANKRUPTCY ESTATE

For each bankruptcy case, the trustee is in charge of what is called a "bankruptcy estate," a sort of temporary company or trust fund set up by the bankruptcy law. The estate technically becomes the legal owner of all of the petitioner's property. If the trustee sells property and makes payments to creditors, those funds are handled through the bankruptcy estate.

The trustee usually releases the estate's claim on at least some property very quickly. Property that is exempt or tied up by liens—and often that's all the property there is—is usually released within two months or less of the filing of the petition. In most cases, the trustee never actually takes possession or control of this kind of property.

In general, a petitioner can continue to go about his or her life and business in a normal manner, even right after a bankruptcy filing. In most routine cases, the petitioner can continue to use and control his or her property, despite the temporary rights of the bankruptcy estate.

The petitioner must still be careful about selling property or making other major transactions until the rights of the estate are cleared up. This is true even with items of property that seem certain to be protected as exempt.

THE U.S. TRUSTEE

The trustee for each Chapter 7 or 13 case is appointed by the "U.S. Trustee." This official is part of the U.S. Justice Department under the jurisdiction of the Attorney General and has certain administrative authority and responsibilities in bankruptcy cases.

At one time, bankruptcy cases were administered almost entirely by judges. That sometimes put the judge in a difficult position. He or she had to be actively involved in cases in ways that other types of judges would not—and still be an impartial decision maker. To avoid that situation, many "nonjudicial" responsibilities have been transferred to individual trustees and the U.S. Trustee system.

The U.S. Trustee is more likely to be actively involved in business reorganization cases and usually does not play a major active role in a routine Chapter 7 or Chapter 13 case.

CHAPTER 9

MORTGAGES AND LIENS

Mortgages and other liens make almost every bankruptcy case unique. Petitioners who seem to have similar property are often affected very differently by bankruptcy, and liens are the reason. The laws that apply to liens in bankruptcy court are complicated, but in many cases they are important.

DEFINITION OF LIEN

Under the Bankruptcy Code, a lien is defined as a "charge or interest in property to secure payment of a debt." Liens that are created voluntarily by contract—home mortgages and car purchase liens, for example—are *security interests.*

Besides security interests, there are two other basic categories of liens. Statutory liens are created automatically by law; tax liens are the most common of these. Judicial liens are created by court order, usually because the creditor has filed suit over an unpaid debt and won a judgment.

Property that is subject to a lien is *encumbered. Collateral* is a common term for property used or offered for use as the subject of a lien. Collateral *secures* the loan connected with the lien.

Lenders are often willing to give loans that they would not otherwise take on or to agree to lower interest rates or other favorable terms if the loan has good collateral that reduces the risk of loss.

The whole point of a lien is to give the creditor special rights to force the sale of the encumbered property, if necessary, to collect the debt that is owed. Creditors enforce their liens by repossessions and foreclosures that take back the collateral to pay off the debt.

Lien rights protect the creditor against the debtor who, without the lien, might be able to keep the property without paying the debt. The creditor is also protected against other creditors because, without the lien, they might be able to get at that property through legal proceedings and use its value to pay their own debts.

The details of how these various rights work in practice depend on the type of lien we are talking about and the particular laws that apply.

KINDS OF LIENS

Liens are used in many different situations, and bankruptcy affects them in different ways.

Real Estate Mortgages   The classic example of a lien is the real estate mortgage, particularly a home loan. Banks or other companies that lend money for purchase of homes protect themselves by taking mortgage liens on the house and land.

There can be more than one lien on the same property. For example, a homeowner may take out a second mortgage loan before the first mortgage is paid off. If the homeowner fails to pay and the property is foreclosed, the first, or "senior," lien is paid off first. The second, or "junior," lien is paid out of any money that is left. The owner gets nothing unless both lenders are paid in full.

Car Loans   Another common example of a voluntary lien is the loan used to buy a car. As with houses and other collateral, a car can be used as collateral for reasons other than the original purchase of the car. The car may also have more than one lien on it at the same time.

> Dave and Beth Wilson bought a camper and paid the loan until they owed only half as much as the camper was worth. Then they used the camper as extra collateral to get a business loan. The bank had a junior lien on the camper to secure the business loan.

Credit Card Liens   Items bought on credit cards and under similar credit plans are usually subject to liens.

Finance companies sometimes take furniture or household goods as collateral for their loans.

Tax Liens   In some situations state and federal tax laws place liens on real estate and other property to help assure that overdue taxes are collected.

Judicial Liens   A judicial lien, granted to a creditor who has won a lawsuit, differs in detail from one state to another, and some kinds of property are protected from being taken (see Chapter 10). The possibility of getting this kind of judicial lien, or judgment lien, and then enforcing it by taking property, is often a creditor's last good shot at collecting.

In most states a creditor who has sued and won a judgment can also garnish the wages of the debtor. Under a wage garnishment, the creditor gets a court order requiring the employer to hold back part of the debtor's wages. The money is then paid either directly to the creditor or into court to be applied to the creditor's account.

WHAT HAPPENS TO LIENS IN BANKRUPTCY

Bankruptcy often does not eliminate lien rights, but there are important exceptions to this general rule. Liens that *are* eliminated by the bankruptcy are said to be "avoided." That's the word used in the law, but it sounds a little clumsy even to lawyers; we'll stick with "canceled." Petitioners can cancel some liens for their own benefit, keeping the property that is thus freed and still discharging the debt. In other situations, the trustee can cancel liens and then sell the property for the benefit of the creditors.

LIENS THE PETITIONER CAN ELIMINATE

A petitioner can usually get free of the following liens in a bankruptcy and keep the collateral without paying the creditor.

Household Goods
A petitioner can eliminate some liens on household goods, personal jewelry, and similar personal property, as well as property used in earning a living. This is allowed if the property would be exempt if it hadn't been tied up by the lien.

> Thomas Martinez took out a finance company loan. He didn't use any of the money to finance new purchases, but the company did require that he list a stereo, a home computer, and some other items as collateral. In Chapter 7, he was able to claim those items as exempt, cancel the liens, and discharge the loan to the finance company.

This cancellation of the lien does not apply to "purchase money security interests"—liens strictly for the purchase price of the property.

The Wilsons bought a new living room set on credit, and the store took a lien on the furniture to secure the money owed. If they were to file bankruptcy while still owing some of that money, they could not cancel that lien. They would have to pay it off, or they would still face the possibility of repossession.

The test is whether you already owned the collateral and then took out a loan on it or are still paying off the original purchase price.

Credit Card Liens

Items bought with a credit card are nearly always subject to a lien until they are paid for. They are "purchase money" liens that cannot be canceled.

Credit card liens, however, are often eliminated in bankruptcy. Most of the items involved are relatively small, and creditors often do not bother to track them down to get reaffirmations or try to repossess collateral.

This is particularly true with general-purpose bank cards. The money is owed to the credit card company, which may not have direct access to store records on exactly what property was purchased. These companies rarely try to enforce lien claims.

Thomas Martinez had several credit cards of various types on which he had bought items that legally might have had liens on them when he filed bankruptcy. His lawyer advised him to wait and see if any of the companies would claim lien rights. One department store did, and Thomas agreed to return a vacuum cleaner and make payments on some other items. He never heard from any of the other companies.

A credit card holder who expects to file bankruptcy and makes large purchases to take advantage of this situation, however, may run into practical trouble—to say nothing of the ethical kind. Either the rules that control dischargeability of debts or the "substantial abuse" dismissal rule could apply.

Judicial Liens

A petitioner can often eliminate a judicial lien. Under some state laws, a creditor's judgment may take the form of a lien on a home or other real estate. If this interferes with a bankruptcy petitioner's claim of homestead exemption rights, the lien may be eliminated.

A business creditor of Dave and Beth sued them and won a judgment. Under their state's law, this gave the creditor a lien on any real estate they owned—for the Wilsons, their home. If they sold the house without a bankruptcy being involved, they would have to pay off that creditor before keeping any money for themselves. But if they filed bankruptcy, they might be able to cancel that judgment lien and eliminate the claim on their home.

PROCEDURE FOR CANCELING LIENS

Liens that can be canceled do not always disappear automatically in bankruptcy. The petitioner must often ask the court to cancel the lien by filing what is called a *motion*. The creditor has a right to contest the motion and try to keep the lien.

Where only a small amount of property is involved, a lawyer may advise that the petitioner not file a motion since the lien might never be pursued anyway. This is a decision that has to be made separately for each case.

WHEN THE TRUSTEE CAN ELIMINATE LIENS AND GET PROPERTY BACK

The bankruptcy trustee is appointed to protect the rights of the petitioner's creditors. Before the debts are discharged, the law requires a close look at the petitioner's property. If there is property that is not exempt and not tied up by liens, it may be sold for cash to be applied to the debts.

The law gives the trustee these powers so that certain basic policies that are behind the Bankruptcy Code can be carried out. These include *priority rules* that decide how creditors will share any money collected from the petitioner's nonexempt property. Special categories (taxes, for example) must be paid first. Anything left over is shared by other creditors in proportion to the size of their claims.

If the law didn't specifically prevent it, a person headed into bankruptcy could do a lot of picking and choosing among creditors. When there is property that would be lost in bankruptcy anyway, the petitioner might pay off selected creditors (or protect them by giving them liens), and only then petition to discharge the rest of the debts.

Another possible strategy is an even greater concern. Bankruptcy petitioners sometimes try to keep property away from creditors altogether by giving it away. Those might be either genuine gifts or else property given under secret agreements that it will be returned later.

To combat these strategies and help assure that creditors are treated fairly, the law gives the trustee a powerful set of legal weapons. The trustee can sometimes cancel liens, recover payments made to creditors before bankruptcy, and undo gifts and certain other transactions.

Money or value from these transactions is then available for the petitioner's creditors, to be divided up under the priority and sharing rules in the bankruptcy law.

Under some sections of the law, in order to reverse a transaction the trustee must prove that the petitioner intended to defraud creditors or evade the priority rules. Other kinds of transactions can be reversed even without any wrongful intention.

The trustee actually takes these kinds of actions in only a small fraction of bankruptcy cases, usually in business bankruptcies. Though such actions are rare in consumer cases, it is important to be aware that a petitioner who gives property away to keep it from creditors, or makes selective payments, can very easily make the situation worse rather than better.

There is nothing necessarily illegal about thinking ahead to the possibility of bankruptcy. People are allowed to know what their legal rights are, including exempt property rights. But "exemption planning" or "bankruptcy planning" is tricky business.

WHAT THE PETITIONER CAN DO ABOUT LIENS AFTER BANKRUPTCY

As we have seen, some liens survive bankruptcy and the creditor still has the right, for example, to the proceeds for the sale of your car, up to the amount you owe.

Bankruptcy does make an important difference: The personal obligation to pay the money is discharged by the bankruptcy. The creditor may go after the property to recover as much of the debt as possible but may not make any other attempts to collect the debt. The petitioner has several options for handling such a situation.

Surrender the Collateral

If the petitioner releases the collateral to the creditor, the problem is solved. The creditor is not entitled to anything more, and the petitioner is then in the clear on that debt.

Thomas Martinez returned the vacuum cleaner to the department store rather than make any further payments on it. That part of his debt to the department store was then discharged.

Continue the Payments

If you have kept up with the payments and the collateral is worth at least as much as the amount owed on it, you may be able simply to continue making the payments, following the terms of the old contract. As long as the creditor is getting the payments due, the bankruptcy doesn't have much practical effect on the contract.

If you proceed this way, there is no risk of being sued later if the collateral declines in value and doesn't cover the debt. The discharge of the personal obligation would still be in effect.

Court decisions about this procedure differ, and it may not be possible in some states if the creditor objects. This should be discussed with an attorney

Reaffirm the Debt

A formal written agreement by a petitioner to keep paying all or part of a debt that would have been discharged is a *reaffirmation agreement.* This is most commonly used when a petitioner wants to keep collateral that is still subject to a lien.

A reaffirmation agreement can be just about any arrangement on which the creditor and petitioner can agree. Many reaffirmation agreements simply extend or modify the original payment terms.

If the collateral is worth a lot less than the amount owed on the loan, the situation is different. Then the reaffirmation is usually for the present resale value of the collateral, not for the full amount of the loan. The petitioner has little incentive to pay more than the property is worth. Since the creditor is not allowed to collect the debt other than from the collateral, some petitioners let the collateral be repossessed and then buy a substitute if they need it.

Creditors will usually ask for reaffirmation for the full balance on the account, but they have good reason to be flexible. A creditor that gets back a used sofa or appliance, for example, can only sell it for whatever it will bring. Creditors are in the money business, not the used collateral business, and the petitioner's money is as good as anybody else's.

Determining the dollar value of the collateral is an important part of negotiating a reaffirmation. If the petitioner and creditor cannot agree, it is possible to have the judge decide, but, because that can be difficult and expensive, it is usually done only when several thousand dollars are at stake. With smaller amounts, both sides are usually better off working something out between them.

Redeem the Collateral

If the petitioner has enough cash, he or she can pay what is owed in full. Of course, people who have just filed bankruptcy are not often in a position to do that, except for very small amounts. The amount that must be paid to redeem collateral is either the amount of the debt or the value of the property, whichever is less.

CHAPTER 10

EXEMPT PROPERTY

One function of our legal system is to enforce debts. If someone owes you money and doesn't pay when it is due, you have certain legal rights to force payment. Through lawsuits and other court procedures, you can seize property and sell it to pay off the debt.

But creditors don't have all the rights. Some kinds of property are "exempt from execution." That means they may not be taken by force of law for payment of most debts, even if the creditor has no other way of getting paid. Exemption laws vary greatly from state to state (see Appendix I), but exempt property is generally what is considered necessary for a normal life for the debtor and his or her family.

This idea of exempt property carries over into bankruptcy. A petitioner is allowed to keep certain kinds and amounts of property as exempt, even while receiving a discharge of debts.

VALUING PROPERTY FOR EXEMPTIONS

Some exemption laws cover a particular type of property up to a certain dollar amount—a car worth up to $1,000, for example. To apply exemption laws, you must know what each item of property is worth—what it would bring in cash if it were sold. That amount is often far less than what it cost or what a replacement would cost.

To analyze the value of property for exemption purposes, any valid liens held by other creditors are deducted. The net value of the item of property, after subtracting liens, is called the owner's *equity*. This equity, rather than the entire value, is the basis for figuring exemptions.

For instance, suppose you own a car you could sell for $2,000. There is a $1,200 lien on the car, so your equity is $800. If the exemption laws allow at least $800 for a car, then your equity is fully exempt. No creditor other than the one with the lien can get permission to seize the car to collect a debt. Your exemption rights do not affect the creditor with the lien, however.

STATE AND FEDERAL EXEMPTION LAWS

There is no uniform national law on exempt property, although the federal Bankruptcy Code does specify exemptions. Each state has its own exemption laws that apply in state court disputes between debtors and creditors when no bankruptcy is involved. In about thirty-five states, those same exemption laws also apply to bankruptcy cases. Petitioners must figure their property rights under state law.

In the other states, petitioners can choose between their state list of exemptions and the separate set of exemption rules contained in the federal Bankruptcy Code. The legislature in each state has the power to allow or forbid that option.

Several large states, including Michigan, Pennsylvania, New Jersey, Texas, Connecticut, and California, do allow a choice. Close to half of all Americans can use the federal exemptions if they wish.

Appendix I summarizes the key provisions of the exemption laws for each state and includes information on whether a choice of exemption lists is allowed in bankruptcy.

EFFECTS OF EXEMPTION RIGHTS

The kinds and amounts of property that are exempt vary widely, depending on where a bankruptcy petitioner lives. Some states allow much more property to be claimed as exempt than others do. As important as these variations are, on the whole they probably make less difference than you might expect.

The main reason is that, not surprisingly, few people consider bankruptcy while they still have substantial assets. More commonly, people try to deal with their debt problems as long as possible by selling whatever assets they have or borrowing against them. Only when that strategy has clearly failed do they consider bankruptcy. By that point, the assets owned free and clear have usually dwindled.

Many bankruptcy petitioners have so little property, or at least so little property free of liens, that what they do have is clearly covered by any set of exemption laws. But when a possible petitioner does have more property, figuring out what property is and is not likely to be exempt is a crucial part of deciding whether to petition for bankruptcy.

EXEMPTIONS FOR A HUSBAND AND WIFE

Under the federal exemptions and also most state laws, a husband and wife are each entitled to a set of exemptions, even if they are filing one joint bankruptcy case. This means that the exemption amounts are, in effect, doubled when the petitioner is actually a couple. When there is a choice of using state or federal exemptions, the husband and wife must make the same choice.

FEDERAL EXEMPTIONS

A review of the exemption rights set out in the federal Bankruptcy Code follows, with some general comments on how various state exemption lists differ from it.

Remember that exemptions are based on equity, not necessarily total value: the amount of valid liens must be deducted to determine exemptible values.

An item can be partly exempt. If you owned a ring worth $5,000 and your state's jewelry exemption is $1,000, a bankruptcy trustee could sell the ring, give you $1,000, and use the rest to pay your creditors.

Homestead

The federal exemptions allow $15,000 for equity in the petitioner's homestead, or primary residence. After paying off mortgages and other liens, that $15,000 can be protected out of the net amount the house would bring if it were sold.

State homestead laws vary widely. Some states have no homestead exemption at all. A few protect homesteads without any dollar limit. Others allow specific dollar values ranging from $1,500 to $100,000.

In some states, a petitioner must file a particular type of registration paper in a state office before the bankruptcy to qualify for a homestead exemption.

When a Chapter 7 petitioner owns a home with a mortgage, it may not be affected one way or the other by the bankruptcy. If the mortgage payments are up to date and the equity is exempt, nothing about a bankruptcy should prevent the petitioner from keeping the home—and the mortgage, of course.

For someone who has a home that is worth more, after mortgages and liens, than can be claimed as exempt, Chapter 7 presents a serious problem: The trustee might take the house and sell it. The petitioner would still get the value of the exemption out of the sale price, but that might not be much consolation. If you are in that situation, a Chapter 13 debt adjustment plan might be a better choice (see page 38).

If the mortgage payments are far enough in default to threaten foreclosure, a Chapter 7 bankruptcy will help only in limited ways. The automatic stay may hold off a foreclosure for a few weeks or months, and discharging other debts through bankruptcy may free up money to use on the mortgage. But you should consult with a lawyer about whether Chapter 13 might produce better results.

Automobile

The federal exemptions allow $2,400 for equity in an automobile. Most states have a similar exemptions, and this amount is fairly typical.

Household Furnishings

The federal exemptions lump household furnishings together with "household goods, wearing apparel, appliances, books, animals, crops, or musical instruments." The amount that can be exempted is $400 per item, up to a total of $8,000. Considering that exemptions are based on as-is resale value and not replacement cost, most people who file for bankruptcy can fit all or virtually all of their household goods into those limits.

All states provide some exemptions for household goods. The details vary widely, but one way or another the contents of an average household are usually fairly well protected. Some laws include specific lists of items, with or without specific dollar limits. Some states get *very* specific. Arizona, for example, allows three living room lamps and one radio alarm clock.

Even if a bankruptcy petitioner does have a few household goods that exceed the exemption limits, it may not make any difference. Trustees will not usually bother trying to take and sell very small amounts of property. If no more than a few hundred dollars would be produced and there is no other nonexempt property, the expenses involved are often more than it is worth to creditors.

When a trustee has a valid claim against personal property that *is* large enough to bother with, he or she may be willing to sell those rights back to the petitioner for whatever amount could be obtained from another buyer. That allows the trustee to get the value of the property for the creditors without the trouble of taking possession and selling it to someone else.

Jewelry

The federal exemptions allow $1,000 for personal jewelry. Many state lists have similar provisions.

Tools of Trade

The federal exemptions allow $1,500 in "implements, professional books, or tools of the trade of the debtor." Most state laws have tools-of-trade exemptions of one sort or another, some for much larger amounts. In some states, the rules vary by occupation.

Life Insurance

The federal exemptions allow $8,000 of the cash value of life insurance plus the other rights in the policy itself. Any loans that have been taken out against the policy are treated as reducing the cash value rather than as a secured debt with the policy as collateral. State laws vary a great deal, but most states have some protection for life insurance.

Health Aids

The federal exemptions cover any amount for "professionally prescribed health aids." Many states have similar provisions. Creditors or trustees rarely try to take this type of property.

Retirement and Pension Benefits

The federal exemptions protect most types of pension plans or accounts "to the extent reasonably necessary for the support of the debtor or any dependent." Most state laws also exempt pension rights, some with the "necessary" limitation and some with no limits.

The laws determining exactly when pension funds are exempt are complicated and unclear, with a web of differing rules and court decisions. In general, most standard pension or retirement accounts are likely to be protected, but those set up privately or belonging to relatively young persons may not be. Individual retirement accounts (IRAs) usually are not exempt in bankruptcy.

Social Security benefits, veteran's benefits, unemployment compensation, disability benefits, and alimony or child support are specifically exempt without any "necessary for support" limitation. These are nearly always exempt under state law as well.

Miscellaneous Property

The federal exemptions allow petitioners to protect a few relatively unusual types of payments to which they may be entitled. These include some types of payments from lawsuits for injuries, life insurance money from the death of a relative, and payments under programs providing reparations to crime victims.

Various state exemption laws also include special provisions covering a variety of different types of property. Many are so specialized that it is hard to imagine them ever coming up in practice. For example, you are in luck if you have:

- Five roosters in Michigan
- A collection of geological specimens in Nevada
- A miner's cabin worth up to $200 in Puerto Rico
- Three swarms of bees in Vermont
- A musket in Iowa
- Six sheep fleeces in New Hampshire

Any Other Property:
The "Wild Card" Exemption

The federal exemptions and a few states allow the petitioner to protect a certain dollar amount of any type of property whatsoever. This so-called "wild card" exemption can be used for additional property of the kinds covered by the specific exemptions, as well as anything else you want to protect, including additional value in a homestead.

The amount allowed under federal law is $800 plus up to $7,500 of any unused portion of the homestead exemption for a total in many cases of $8,300.

The flexibility of this rule is one of the most attractive features of the federal exemptions. It often allows people with limited amounts of property to protect it without having to fit it into certain narrow categories.

TENANCY BY THE ENTIRETY
UNDER STATE LAW

"Tenancy by the entirety (or entireties)" is an old and complicated type of co-ownership of property between a husband and wife. It applies usually to real estate but sometimes to other property as well. It was developed centuries ago as part of the common law of England, and is still recognized in many states. Such property sometimes has special protection from creditors that is carried over into bankruptcy as an additional exemption.

EXEMPTION PLANNING

Selling nonexempt property to buy exempt property or transferring value to exempt property in some other way is sometimes called "exemption planning" or "bankruptcy planning."

Court decisions do not agree on whether exemption planning is proper. When a court rules against it, the result can be denial of exempt property rights or denial of discharge of debts.

A person who may be headed for bankruptcy and may have a significant amount of nonexempt property to protect should consult a bankruptcy lawyer before moving assets around in hopes of making them exempt. Do-it-yourself exemption planning can lead to big trouble.

CHAPTER 11

HANDLING DEBTS WITHOUT BANKRUPTCY

With a little knowledge, debt problems can often be handled without resorting to anything as drastic as bankruptcy. This is especially true of commercial debts—those owed to banks, finance companies, department stores, credit card companies, and the like.

STRATEGIES CREDITORS FOLLOW

Even when a debtor is behind on payments, creditors are not always quick to file lawsuits. Lawsuits cost money for legal and filing costs, and under some circumstances a creditor must go through specific steps before being allowed to sue. Therefore, creditors nearly always try very hard to collect their accounts out of court. In addition to normal billing, out-of-court collection includes an array of techniques: notices, final notices, telephone calls, collection agency notices, lawyer's letters, and "final final" notices.

All of those involve demanding or asking for payment, as distinguished from legally forcing it. Without going to court first, most creditors can't do anything *except* ask and demand.

CREDITORS WITH SPECIAL PRE-LAWSUIT POWERS

There are some categories of creditors who don't have to go to court to have a powerful effect on your life. If you can't pay all your bills, these go near the top of the list.

Utilities

Generally speaking, if you have an overdue bill with a business, that business does not have to continue dealing with you or selling to you. But for most businesses, cutting you off isn't overly effective. You can just go to a competitor.

It *is,* however, effective in the case of utilities. Customers can rarely switch to another telephone, gas, or electric company. The ability to cut off service is a powerful collection device for such creditors.

Car Loan Lenders

A good lien puts the creditor in a strong position. It works with car loans as well as with almost anything else.

Collateral exists so a creditor may repossess property if a loan is not repaid. In most states, a creditor can do that without going to court first—but only under certain conditions. Without a court order, the creditor may not go into a home or onto private property without permission to get the collateral.

Most kinds of collateral for personal loans are things that are kept in the home so, as a practical matter, court action is usually needed for repossession. The exception is when the creditor can get easy access to the collateral—by finding it in a public place, for example.

One kind of collateral that is hard to avoid leaving in a public place is a car. Creditors can and do repossess cars simply by taking them. They may use some of the same methods as car thieves do—duplicate keys or hot wiring—or they may have the car towed.

If you are behind on a car loan, either be very careful where you leave your car or make very sure you know how your local repossession laws work.

Tax Authorities

The Internal Revenue Service and other tax collectors have legal ways to collect debts in civil tax claims, such as when a truthful return was filed but the tax shown on the return was not paid. (Filing a false return and not filing when required are crimes that can lead to fines or jail.)

A tax lien can tie up your home or other real estate without court action. Businesses can be shut down for failure to pay taxes. Even if you are not in business, taxes are a special problem because of the high interest and penalties and because most taxes are not discharged in bankruptcy.

Student Loans

Some types of student loans can be collected by seizure of tax refunds without a court order.

Child Support Debts

Certain child support debts can also be collected by wage garnishment and seizure of tax refunds without a court order. In addition, there is a greater danger of going to jail on a contempt-of-court order for failure to pay child support than for almost any other type of debt.

DEALING WITH DEBT COLLECTION

There are several good strategies for dealing with more typical creditors, those who must go to court before they have the right to garnish wages or seize property.

In dealing with creditors you should always take honesty and reasonableness as far as they will go. If you explain why your account is in default, you may be able to persuade the creditor to allow you more time for payment or to make other concessions.

But not always. Creditors and individual collection agents come in all varieties. Some are reasonable; others rely on threats and intimidation—though opinions may differ about where aggressive but fair debt collection ends and intimidation begins.

Whatever their style, never make the mistake of letting collection agents be your legal or financial advisers. Their interests and priorities are totally different from yours. Furthermore, they are not usually lawyers or consumers' rights specialists. Even a sincere collection agent may not really know much about his or her company's legal rights, let alone yours.

You need to know what the creditor can do, both legally and practically, before you can deal effectively with debt collection. You also should know how you can respond to creditors. If you don't, you have no way to sort out real danger from bluff and bluster.

When, Where, and How to Talk to Creditors

During out-of-court collection, it is your right to set the rules of communication. In particular, no law says you have to talk on the telephone with a creditor—or anyone else—if you don't want to.

If you are convinced that persuading creditors to give you just a little more time will make a difference in your situation, you have reason to be particularly nice to them on the phone. In general, though, there is no reason to assume anything will come out differently even if you insist on communicating only by mail.

If you don't want to discuss a debt by telephone, say so and suggest that the caller send you a letter. Understand that telephone collectors are trained to be forceful and will not always politely break off a conversation when asked. If you want to discourage future calls, you have to be prepared to be firm. It won't help to argue with the collector for five minutes and then say, "I don't want to talk to you." Hanging up on someone who is still talking is bad manners in most situations, but with collection agents you may have to. To make your point, you have to cut the conversation short.

Does Making Small Payments Help?

You can always make smaller payments than the creditor tells you to or than the original contract requires. What creditors say in advance about what payments they will accept and what they will actually do are often two different things.

Debt collectors routinely tell customers that they *must* pay in full immediately or must pay some specific amount; it's part of standard collection psychology. A collector may tell you not to bother making payments of less than a certain amount. However, this rarely means that the creditor will actually send smaller payments back if you make them or that those payments won't make a difference in what the creditor does next.

Small payments do not necessarily stop a creditor from going to court. If you are a dollar short and a day beyond the grace period, the creditor can start legal proceedings. But creditors almost never move that quickly, especially on consumer debts. If you stop making payments completely, a lawsuit is likely to follow sooner or later. But if you are still making payments, even small ones, the creditor has a tougher decision to make and may hold off on legal action.

Making smaller payments may allow you to get through temporary financial difficulties. The key word is "temporary." If your debts are too large to be handled with the income available, making smaller payments is no solution. Most consumer debts carry high interest rates. If you can't pay enough on your total debt load both to cover the interest and to reduce the balance due, you are losing ground and headed for even worse trouble.

Harassment Laws

There are laws controlling debt collection practices and prohibiting harassment. You may sue creditors who use certain extreme collection tactics.

A federal law, for instance, strictly regulates the techniques collection agencies may use for consumer debts. The following are among the things they may not do:

- Call before 8 A.M. or after 9 P.M.
- Use threats of violence or obscene or profane language
- Publish lists of people who owe money
- Misrepresent who is calling
- Threaten to take steps other than proper actions that are actually planned
- Communicate by postcard (and risk exposing private matters)
- Refuse to provide verification of a debt on proper request

This particular law does not apply to in-house collectors working directly for the creditor, but many other federal, state, and local laws do.

Harassment suits are almost never a solution to debt problems, however, and even perfectly legal debt collection tactics can leave a customer feeling harassed.

Refinancing and Consolidation Loans

Creditors may suggest—or demand—that you borrow money somewhere else to pay them. You would be wise to take that advice with a grain of salt. Collection agents are out to collect their own accounts as quickly as possible and are not much concerned about helping you straighten out your finances. This makes them an extremely bad source of advice on whether to borrow from somebody else.

Sometimes it *is* a good idea to take out a new loan to refinance a debt or to consolidate several debts. You might be better off, for example, if the new loan has a lower interest rate or lower total payments that would help make your finances manageable.

Before taking out a loan to pay other debts, you need to do some very careful figuring and thinking—about interest rates, total payments, your income, and your entire financial situation. If you don't feel confident about doing that analysis, discuss it with a professional debt counselor, an accountant, or someone else who is knowledgeable and objective.

If you are thinking of borrowing from a friend or relative rather than a bank or other financial institution, you should analyze the situation much the same way. Think very clearly about whether you will be able to repay the loan. There is a huge difference between wanting to pay it back—or planning, intending, or hoping to pay it back—and actually being able to do it when the time comes.

If the loan is really a gift in disguise, obviously you and the lender/giver should be on the same wavelength about that. If it is truly a loan, consider carefully whether you are solving your financial problems or just dragging a friend or relative into them. Financial entanglements can damage good relationships. If you are going into a private loan arrangement, do it with your eyes open. Make full disclosure to the lender and set up a practical repayment plan as quickly as possible.

The same is true if the friend or relative is cosigning a loan, rather than lending you the money directly. A cosigner must pay the debt if you don't. There is always some chance it will work out that way, hard as you may try to convince yourself that it can't. Don't get into such a situation unless you and the cosigner are ready to deal with the consequences.

DEBT PROBLEMS, SPENDING PROBLEMS

Too much debt often comes at least in part from bad spending habits or other problems with handling money. When spending habits are a problem, bankruptcy by itself is not a complete solution. Either counseling or a major effort at self-analysis is needed.

Changing spending habits is fairly simple for some people once they put their minds to it. For others it can be psychologically wrenching and a difficult lifestyle change. A husband and wife who are otherwise compatible may have learned very different attitudes and approaches about money, and the resulting conflicts sometimes threaten to cause both bankruptcy and divorce.

If you believe you might benefit from analyzing your approach to money issues, try to find a counselor who is skilled in dealing with such issues. You may be able to get a referral from a government social services agency, a psychologist, or another mental health care provider.

WHEN THE LAWSUITS START

The rules of debt collection change when a creditor stops threatening and actually files a lawsuit. Filing suit puts a creditor on the way to possible wage garnishment, real estate liens, and seizure of property.

The first key to dealing with a lawsuit is to realize it is happening. The legal documents that notify you about a lawsuit vary from one place to another but are nearly always some form of papers called a *summons and complaint.* The papers may be delivered in person by a police officer or process server or may come by mail.

The summons tells the person being sued, the *defendant,* that the lawsuit has been started. The complaint tells the creditor's story in a brief form and tells the court what the creditor, known as the *plaintiff,* wants done about it. In a debt collection suit, the creditor wants a judgment formally declaring that an amount of money is owed. The summons and complaint usually come stapled together; in a simple case they may be on a single piece of paper.

If you are not familiar with legal documents, the summons and complaint may not be easy to follow. The summons tells you what to do if you want to fight the claim: either appear in court at a particular time or respond in writing to the court and to the creditor or creditor's lawyer.

That written answer is subject to very specific legal rules, and those rules are not usually explained in the lawsuit papers. Trying to answer a lawsuit by letter without understanding the rules is dangerous. It's not as bad as ignoring a lawsuit completely, but it's close.

The single most important bit of information you must extract from the summons and complaint is simply that you are being sued. Unless you are absolutely sure you know what is going on and how to handle it, you should talk to a lawyer immediately. This is true whether you admit that the claim being made is correct or believe you have good grounds for fighting it. It is also true whether the suit involves a debt or something else—an accident or a family matter. Ignoring the lawsuit guarantees that the creditor will quickly win a judgment against you and that you will have no say in the matter.

You usually have ten to thirty days to respond to the lawsuit; the summons should give you that information, although it does not always appear in clear form. The time allowed is nearly always short enough that you need to move quickly to protect your rights.

LAWSUITS AND BANKRUPTCY

Most people who are sued resolve the situation by paying the amount claimed, compromising the lawsuit, or successfully defending against it.

But for others, being sued is the event that causes them to investigate bankruptcy. Bankruptcy affects lawsuits in two basic ways. First, filing for bankruptcy triggers the automatic stay order against creditors. This court order immediately halts virtually any lawsuit, often permanently. If you do owe the money being claimed, have no good basis for contesting the lawsuit, but can't pay the money, bankruptcy may be the only way to prevent the creditor from getting and enforcing a judgment against you. The rest of your financial situation must, of course, be taken into account in that decision.

Second, the possibility of bankruptcy may improve your negotiating position. It may help if you let a creditor know that you are aware of your bankruptcy rights and might use them if no settlement is reached. Creditors may become more flexible about the amount of money or the payment terms they will accept as a compromise.

This strategy doesn't work as well or as often as you might think. Many creditors have a policy that they won't risk being bluffed about bankruptcy filings. They take the attitude that if you file for bankruptcy, then you do, but until then they'll press ahead.

A bankruptcy discharge eliminates a debt, even if a lawsuit was filed and a judgment has been granted on it. There are only two situations in which a creditor has more rights in bankruptcy because it has received a judgment: First, when a judgment has become a lien on specific property, the lien may or may not survive bankruptcy (see page 73). Second, a judgment prevents the debtor from contesting the amount owed again in the bankruptcy court. That rarely makes any difference in a Chapter 7. In a Chapter 13, it has an effect on how much the creditor is entitled to be paid under the repayment plan.

WHEN THE CREDITOR IS WRONG

Most of our discussion of collection so far has assumed that the creditor is right that you owe the money and is correct about the amount. If you genuinely believe a creditor is wrong about a claim being made against you, you have some other things to worry about.

When the creditor first bills you for the disputed amount, you should state as clearly and simply as possible why the bill is wrong. If bills keep coming, you may need to repeat the explanation. Handle everything in writing and keep copies of all papers.

If you have reason to believe that the creditor has violated a consumer protection law, you can and should file a report with the appropriate agency. What that is varies from state to state; the local prosecuting attorney's office is probably a good place to start.

If the creditor won't back down, and especially if a lawsuit is filed, you should think long and hard about a possible compromise. Legal battles over relatively small amounts of money can easily leave both sides worse off. Be realistic about how much is at stake and how much time and effort you are willing to devote to the issue. Be aware that the creditor will often have more resources to fight with than you do.

If you can't avoid the fight or are sure that you don't want to, you have one very important advantage. The creditor must bring documents and other evidence to court to prove its case, or it loses. Even if the creditor has been bluffing up to that point, the bluff usually won't work on a judge.

But if you want your day in court, you must be all the more careful. You have to know what the legal procedures are, and to take the right steps at the right time. You may not get a second chance.

If you dispute one or two debts but are headed into bankruptcy anyway because of other debts, it is probably pointless to fight over those one or two. Bankruptcy discharges both disputed and undisputed debts. In a Chapter 7, it usually doesn't much matter if the creditor's claim is right or wrong. If it does make a difference how much a particular creditor is owed, such as in a Chapter 13, that can be decided by the bankruptcy judge.

CHAPTER 12

"BAD CREDIT RATING"

"**D**oesn't it mean I'll never get credit again?"

I have been asked that question by hundreds of people who were considering bankruptcy. For many of them, credit rating worries seemed to be the hardest part of facing up to the possibility of bankruptcy.

Many people with very serious debt problems never even look into bankruptcy because they think that they will pay too high a price in damage to their credit ratings. And that idea is encouraged by the credit industry—banks, loan companies, and other lenders.

Let's take a closer look at whether those worries are justified.

WHAT IS A CREDIT RATING?

We hear and read a lot about credit ratings, usually without anyone taking a careful look at just what those words mean. There is no central computer that decides who gets credit. There are such things as credit bureaus, which are businesses that collect information on the financial activities of just about everybody. The bureaus then sell that information to lenders and other businesses as "credit reports."

Three major national credit companies—TRW, Trans Union, and Equifax—either own or provide the raw data for most credit bureaus across the country. Credit reports can include records on debt repayment, defaults, repossessions or foreclosures, employment, and other financial matters, including bankruptcy. Credit bureaus have so much information and sell it in so many different ways that some experts consider them a threat to our privacy. They do not, however, decide who gets credit. The individual stores and lenders do that.

For some employment applications or large loan reviews, there are no time limits, but most negative items of information can be included in standard reports for only seven years. Bankruptcy filings can be reported for ten years.

You have a right to examine your own credit records, to challenge incorrect information, and to add an explanatory statement to the record if necessary. If you have been denied credit in the last thirty days due to a credit report, you can get a copy free. Otherwise, there is usually a small charge. To find the most logical agency from which to get the report, try asking businesses with whom you deal or that operate in your area what agency they use. If that doesn't work, look in your local yellow pages under "Credit Agencies" or "Credit Reporting Agencies."

A report from a bureau is only part of the credit process. Each bank, store, finance company, or other possible credit source makes its own decisions about giving loans or selling on credit. They use information supplied on your application, credit reports, and sometimes their own investigations. Each company has its own procedures and policies for deciding whether to give credit and in what amount.

We have been led to believe that, week by week and month by month, our bill-paying habits build a credit record and rating. That record, good or bad, is supposed to follow us and to control our finances and ability to get credit, if not forever, then certainly for many long years.

There may be a grain of truth in that, but there is a barrelful of myth.

WHAT HAVE YOU DONE *LATELY*?

Your ability to get credit at any given time is based almost entirely on the hard facts of your *current* financial situation—your property and assets, your other debts, and, most important, the size and stability of your income. Owning a home is considered a good sign of stability, even beyond its direct financial value. Whether you have recently been paying on time on your active loans and charge accounts, if any, may also be a factor.

Your past record counts for something, but it gets old quickly. The current facts are so important that they tend to crowd out anything, positive or negative, that is over and done with. That includes past history of late payments, court judgments that were eventually paid, foreclosures, or repossessions—and bankruptcy.

A sharp drop in income can undo years of building a "good credit rating" overnight. It works the other way too; if you have a good income, a troubled past can fade very quickly, especially if it does not show up as debts you still owe.

HOW HARD IS GETTING CREDIT, REALLY?

The worry about credit ratings is also exaggerated because credit is not particularly hard to come by in the United States. Most of us could get far more credit than a financial advisor with our best interests at heart would ever recommend we take. The credit industry solemnly warns us not to damage our credit ratings by missing a payment. However, they also bombard us with ads telling us that we should borrow more, and how easy it is to do so.

Lenders and sellers are definitely *not* looking for reasons to turn down every applicant so that they will not have to do any business. They may sometimes like to give that impression when it suits their purposes, but it isn't so.

HOW BANKRUPTCY AFFECTS FUTURE CREDIT

How do you know if bankruptcy will affect your ability to get credit in the future? There is no specific answer. Future credit decisions will depend mostly on your future financial situation, and nobody can predict that accurately.

If you have reached the point of even considering bankruptcy, you almost certainly have or are headed for a less-than-perfect credit record, no matter what you do. If it isn't bankruptcy, then it will probably be defaults, lawsuits, judgments, and so on. It is hard to say whether one or the other is clearly worse.

Finally, a bankruptcy usually makes an immediate *favorable* change in your financial status. It eliminates many of your debts and assures that you will not file Chapter 7 again for at least six years. To some creditors—the more cynical or the more rational, as you prefer—that actually tends to make a recent bankruptcy petitioner a *better* risk.

CHAPTER 13 AND CREDIT RATINGS

Suppose a particular store or lender does count a past bankruptcy against credit applicants, reasoning that bankruptcy is a sign of irresponsibility. If that were the case, you would think a Chapter 13 would concern them less. If the applicant took on a payment plan, one would think that would be better than if he or she had asked for a complete discharge of debts. In fact, some petitioners choose Chapter

13 over Chapter 7 because they hope it will help them with future credit.

But it doesn't always work out like that. For a Chapter 13 filer to end up with better credit later on, several things have to happen:

The person making the credit decision must have clear information that the bankruptcy case was a Chapter 13, rather than a Chapter 7. That loan officer must also know what part of the debts were paid; it could have been 2 percent or 100 percent, or anything in between. And the loan officer must understand bankruptcy law well enough to know what those facts mean.

Unfortunately, not everyone in the credit business is well informed about such matters. To cite just one example, new credit reports from a computerized national system in recent years were still using bankruptcy-related terminology that had been out of date since 1978.

There is another complication: For three years or more, the Chapter 13 petitioner has an active case in bankruptcy court and is under the court's jurisdiction. That does not necessarily prevent him or her from receiving new credit, but it does tend to make lenders nervous. A Chapter 7, by comparison, is usually over and done with in four or five months.

In general, creditors seem to take the view that either an account was paid in full, with interest, or it wasn't. A Chapter 13 or other compromise settlement gets lumped with a Chapter 7 under "wasn't."

Add those things together, and the extra investment in a Chapter 13 looks like a very expensive way of trying to buy a better credit rating. Chapter 13 may be a good idea for many other reasons, but this one is shaky.

LET LENDERS COMPETE
FOR YOUR BUSINESS

If you believe in an all-powerful credit rating that will follow you anywhere, you may overlook a simple and effective answer to credit record problems: shopping for credit when you need it.

There are a lot of banks, savings and loans, credit companies, finance companies, and other sources of credit in our society. Having a credit application turned down by one does not necessarily mean that you will be rejected by another down the street. Persistence in seeking out credit may often be an easier and more effective way of getting credit than doing battle with a credit bureau. The goal, after all, is the credit, not the rating.

If you need credit, try letting the free enterprise system work for you. Let companies compete for your business. But remember that not all loans are the same. Keep a close eye on the interest rate and on what, if any, property you are being asked to put up as collateral. Shop as carefully for loans as you would for cars or appliances.

THE CREDIT PREOCCUPATION

It is ironic that many bankruptcy petitioners worry so much about their credit ratings, when easy credit has sometimes contributed to their financial problems. I sometimes think of a poor swimmer splashing frantically in the deep end of the pool and in danger of going under—but unwilling to call for help for fear of not being allowed back in the next day.

When the immediate problems are serious enough, you have to deal with them head on. The possible longer-term consequences, even potentially severe ones, may have to go on the back burner.

Credit is not a necessity for a normal life. Some people go through their entire lives without any credit cards or loans, except perhaps to buy a house. If you have had financial problems related to use of credit, learning to get along without it may be a much better use of your time and energy than plotting to get back into the borrowing business. Not having a charge card is a good way to keep from charging. Going without a credit card for a while may be a good way to start controlling your debts.

SUPPOSE IT WERE TRUE

Just for the exercise, let's suppose it were true that bankruptcy ruins your credit. What if a bankruptcy on your record really does keep you from getting credit afterwards, even if your income and financial situation are strong?

My opinion is that most people who chose to file bankruptcy would still be justified in doing so, even under those conditions. The value of getting free of unmanageable debts would usually outweigh the loss of future credit opportunities. And many people would find that being forced to do without credit was more good than bad in the long run.

If buying a house were made much harder, that would be a serious drawback for some people, but if you have the income for the mortgage payments, a way can almost always be found. Try to save longer for a larger down payment, or find a "seller-financed" arrangement. In any event, there is a good chance that still being in serious debt would be an even bigger obstacle to home ownership than bankruptcy would.

Getting credit depends largely on your current situation. A misinformed and exaggerated preoccupation with future credit is a drawback to making an intelligent decision about bankruptcy. Bankruptcy may not be for you, but concern about future credit should rarely be the deciding factor.

PERSONAL BANKRUPTCY AND THE SMALL BUSINESS OWNER

This book focuses primarily on consumers who earn wages or salaries rather than business owners or the self-employed. The actual line between the two can be rather fuzzy, however. Business-related debts can arise from a part-time sideline business, or even from managing a business without owning it.

Anyone who wants to stay in control of his or her finances should know something about small business, and the debt risks that go with it. With a good understanding of these subjects, some people might actually be *more* willing to take the risk of going into business.

BUSINESS STRUCTURES

Ownership of a business is usually set up in one of three basic ways: sole proprietorship, partnership, or corporation. The kind and degree of debt risks that the owners face depend on which type it is.

SOLE PROPRIETORSHIP

A business that is owned by one person and not incorporated is a sole proprietorship. The main advantage of this setup is simplicity.

A sole proprietor directly owns the business property— equipment, inventory, and other assets—on the same legal basis as his or her home, household goods, or other personal property. The owner also personally owes the business debts, the same as personal ones.

When a sole proprietor uses a trade name or business name, it is technically another name for the owner.

A sole proprietor needs to keep careful, separate financial records for the business. The business is treated as a separate unit for many tax purposes. This is true even of a one-person business with no employees.

When a sole proprietor is facing bankruptcy, the choices are the same as for an individual who hasn't been in business. He or she can file for a discharge under Chapter 7; for a debt adjustment under Chapter 13 (subject to the limit on total debts); and also in some cases under Chapter 11 or the other business reorganization chapters.

Most sole proprietors who file under Chapter 7 have gone out of business or are about to do so. It is legally possible, however, for a proprietor to discharge business debts under Chapter 7 and stay in business, or go back into business.

PARTNERSHIP

A business that is owned by more than one person and not incorporated is a "partnership." Under a partnership, the property and debts of the business are covered by different legal rules than the ones covering the owners' personal finances. Each partner is still personally liable for the debts of the business if the partnership doesn't pay.

That description applies to what is called a "general partnership." There is a slightly different setup called a "limited partnership" that combines some of the features of a partnership and a corporation. There is at least one general partner, and one or more limited partners who are much like stockholders in a corporation. Limited partners are generally not personally liable for business debts.

A partnership can file a bankruptcy petition separately from the owners. It can file under Chapter 7, or under Chapter 11 and the other business reorganization chapters.

If one of the partners goes into bankruptcy, the partnership can legally continue in business. Depending on the bankrupt partner's assets, the partner's bankruptcy trustee may be entitled to his or her share of partnership profits.

The individual partner who is filing for bankruptcy should notify the creditors of the partnership. They are potentially personal creditors as well.

A partnership cannot file under Chapter 13. In practice, however, a small business such as one owned by a husband and wife that is technically a partnership may be able to get the benefits of Chapter 13 if the owners file individual cases.

CORPORATION

A corporation is a type of organization formed by filing incorporation papers with a state government. For most purposes, a corporation is legally treated as if it were a separate person, distinct from the owners (called "stockholders"). A corporation can own property and owe money in its own name. It can sue or be sued, and even be convicted of a crime.

Virtually all large businesses, and many small ones, are set up as corporations.

Corporations are not hard to establish. Operating one properly to run a small business, however, is more complicated than using the other forms of business organization.

A major owner of a small business corporation can easily have several different legal relationships with the corporation at the same time. The same person can be a stockholder, member of the board of directors, officer, employee, creditor and debtor. All those relationships need to be kept straight, or legal and financial chaos may ensue.

Limited Liability   An owner of a corporation, even a sole owner with 100 percent of the shares, is not automatically liable for the corporation's debts. An ordinary creditor that fails to collect from the corporation usually can't touch the owners or their personal property. This so-called "limited liability" is one of the major advantages of setting up a business as a corporation.

It is interesting to note that there is a similarity between filing bankruptcy on personal debts, and escaping corporate debts through the limited liability rule. There is room for a good argument that the two laws serve very similar purposes.

There are people who imagine that they would never consider filing for bankruptcy, but would not hesitate to use corporations to do much the same thing—that is, obtain the benefits of owning a business while preserving the option of walking away from its debts if necessary.

Not-so-limited Liability   Any major owner of a small business corporation still runs a significant risk of personally owing business debts. Several kinds of debts cause problems that the limited liability rule doesn't fix:

- Withholding taxes or sales taxes that a business is supposed to collect for the government are the personal responsibility of the individuals running the company. We will discuss this problem in more detail.
- Banks or key suppliers often demand and get personal guarantees from the owners as a condition of granting loans or credit to the corporation.

- Carelessness about using the corporate name, and being sure that creditors know they are dealing with a corporation, can lead to personal liability for the owner.
- Even a creditor that legally has a claim only against the corporation may try to collect from the owners anyway— either by honest mistake or otherwise. The corporate owners need to be careful about denying and defending incorrect personal claims, especially if the creditor sues on the debt. If the creditor wins a default judgment against an owner, then the owner *becomes* personally liable, whether that was true originally or not.
- Some environmental protection laws can create personal liability for corporate stockholders.

Corporate Bankruptcy A corporation can file under Chapter 7, as well as Chapter 11 and the other business reorganization chapters. A corporation cannot receive a discharge of debts under Chapter 7, so it is next to impossible for a corporation to file Chapter 7 and stay in business. Corporations cannot file under Chapter 13.

The owners of a corporation, or even a 100 percent owner, do not *directly* own the inventory, equipment or other property of the corporation. The corporation itself owns those things, and the individuals own stock, or shares of ownership, in the corporation.

When a *stockholder* files bankruptcy, those shares of ownership are property that must be listed in the personal bankruptcy. The shares of stock are then classified in that case as any other property would be. They may be encumbered by liens, exempt, or available to be sold off for the benefit of the stockholder's creditors.

When a Chapter 7 petitioner has been a major owner of a small business corporation that failed, the owner is wise to see that all creditors of the corporation get notice of the bankruptcy. Many of those corporate creditors may have no legal claim against the owner personally, so strictly speaking they are not involved in the personal bankruptcy. But it is not always clear which creditors do or don't *claim* some rights against the owner. It is a good precaution to see that any such claims are taken care of by the personal bankruptcy.

The "Limited Liability Company"   Many states in recent years have authorized a slightly different type of business organization called the limited liability company, often abbreviated LLC. For most purposes it is similar to a corporation. Under the tax laws, however, it is generally treated like a partnership. That decreases the chances that business profits will be taxed twice, once at the business level and again when dividends are paid to the owners, as can happen with a corporation.

For tax purposes, there is no automatic advantage to any particular type of business organization. The tax laws apply differently to different situations, and change often. A small business owner should get professional advice before adopting or switching to a particular type of business structure.

THE WITHHOLDING TAX TRAP

Withholding taxes and sales taxes are a particular danger for the owners and managers of small businesses of all types.

Any business with employees must withhold income and social security taxes from its payroll, and then pay them to the government. In many states, businesses that make retail sales of any kind must also collect and pay over sales taxes. This tax money is legally classified as government property that the business is required to protect as a trust fund until it is paid in.

Some small businesses come up with the bright idea that if the people who seemed to be employees were actually independent contractors, it would save a bundle on things like withholding taxes. It's not that easy. Even if both the employer and employee agree in writing to the independent contractor arrangement, the government may not go along. Strict requirements have to be met, or the supposed independent contractors are legally employees anyway, and the payroll taxes are still owed—perhaps including back taxes.

If withholding taxes are not paid over to the government when they are supposed to be, the government can charge the unpaid amount personally against whatever individual or individuals were responsible for seeing that the taxes got paid. This can be done under any type of business structure, including a corporation. Even employees who are not owners are sometimes held liable this way for some kinds of business taxes.

When a small business comes on hard times, tough choices have to be made. Paying employees, suppliers or the landlord may seem more urgent, so the trust fund taxes are sometimes allowed to slide. The wheels that are squeaking louder at the moment get the grease.

It's a bad idea. These taxes carry heavy interest and penalties, and they are one of the very few types of debts that can't be discharged or reduced without the creditor's consent in any type of bankruptcy. They are worse in this way than one's own personal income taxes.

These trust funds are the last place from which a business should "borrow" money—but sometimes the first place it does. If a business can't afford to stay current on these taxes, it can't afford to stay in business.

TAKING RISKS

We are painting a bleak picture here of the debt risks of going into business. Fortunately, this is by no means the whole story. A great deal of satisfaction and independence flow from owning a successful business.

Also, I suspect that some people would be *more* willing to

go into business if they knew and understood more about the financial risks and how to control them. The extent to which the bankruptcy laws provide a safety net of sorts is part of that picture.

I think it would be a realistic, common sense idea for anyone starting a business, or thinking about it, to talk with a lawyer about bankruptcy. That should come under the heading of contingency planning—limiting the damage if the business doesn't go well, as all too many small businesses don't.

Large corporations don't start new ventures without carefully considering the downside risks. A pilot, by analogy, does not take off *expecting* to make an emergency landing—but one with any sense still prepares very carefully for that possibility.

Unfortunately, very few small business owners ever have that discussion until it is too late.

CHAPTER 14

THREE ENDINGS

Now that we've examined the bankruptcy process, let's go back to the three situations we started out with.

Serious as his financial problems were, the surprise of receiving divorce papers kept Thomas Martinez from concentrating very much on his debts for a while. Finding a place to live and coming to terms with things like scheduling visits with his children took priority.

As soon as his life settled down, Tom asked the lawyer he had hired for the divorce what he should do about all the debts. Together they decided that he would have to file either a Chapter 7 or a Chapter 13 because there was no other way to stop the wage garnishments.

A close look at Tom's budget showed that in a Chapter 13, he would be able to pay only about 20 percent of the amounts he owed on unsecured debts, even over three years and without further interest. And even making those limited payments would be a strain. Since there was no particular legal or financial advantage for him in choosing Chapter 13, he decided to file Chapter 7.

There were some rough spots during the bankruptcy case. A creditor filed an objection, claiming that the loan application Tom had originally made had not been truthful. There were also some negotiations about liens on the car and various household goods.

Tom got through those hurdles and received his discharge of debts. His legal obligations to pay the credit card balances were gone, as were some smaller debts. Some of the debts he still did have to pay had been reduced in amount. He did not lose any property that wasn't covered by liens.

Bankruptcy left Tom a man with fewer problems and a better opportunity to deal with the ones that remained—sorting out the divorce, supporting his children, and rebuilding his life and finances.

The arrival of lawsuits on both student loans and medical bills sent Susan Novak to a lawyer. When she explained that she could not count on getting financial help from her family, other choices were explored.

The first possibility was to take each debt separately and try to negotiate the best deal possible. If each creditor would accept small enough payments, Sue might just be able to work her way out of the situation. Unfortunately, the strategy would fail if even one creditor pushed ahead with a lawsuit and other legal action. The risk of that happening was too great, considering the dollar amounts involved; Sue had to do something to stop the lawsuits.

The second possibility was a Chapter 7 bankruptcy. Filing a Chapter 7 would eliminate the medical bills and a few miscellaneous bills—about half of her debts in total dollar amount. All of Sue's property would be protected as exempt, but the student loans would not be discharged; they would fall within the exceptions that apply in Chapter 7 cases.

The third possibility was Chapter 13. Based on her income and expenses, Sue could propose a debt adjustment plan that would pay something more than half her debts over three years. The plan would need to pay the student loans in full because they could not be discharged. If the judge approved it—and Sue's lawyer thought he would—she would be protected from lawsuits and garnishments during the three years. At the end, the remaining debts would be discharged.

It was a close call for Sue. The total amount of money that she would end up paying in Chapter 13 would be about the same as the student loans she would still have to pay after a Chapter 7. The deciding factor was the complete protection from legal action that a Chapter 13 would give her. After a Chapter 7, if she couldn't work out terms on the student loans, she might still be back in court and facing wage garnishments.

Sue filed for Chapter 13, and her repayment plan was approved. At last report, her health was better, her finances had stabilized, and she had started writing short stories again.

The closing of their store left Dave and Beth Wilson with a complicated situation.

Within a couple of months, Dave had a good job managing a store similar to the one they had owned. Though the family's combined income was less than when the business had been booming, they were not doing too badly. They had cut back, but they still had their house and cars and were able to make the payments.

They also had more debts than they could hope to pay. Far and away the largest chunk was owed to the government for payroll taxes. Some smaller amounts were due for back rent and bills to suppliers. Most of the bank loans had been paid by selling out the inventory of the store, but there was still a small balance on that debt as well.

Dave and Beth considered both a Chapter 7 and a Chapter 13. Either one would have helped them in some ways but left them with some problems. Chapter 7 would discharge the nontax debts but would have no effect on the taxes. Chapter 13 would not keep the Wilsons from having to pay the taxes in full. Accumulation of new interest and penalties could be stopped and past penalties reduced, but a trustee's commission would be added. The other debts could be reduced, perhaps substantially, but that would reduce their total debt load only slightly.

One major advantage of a Chapter 13 would be protection from lawsuits while payments were being made through the court according to the plan.

After weighing the options, the Wilsons decided not to file either a Chapter 7 or a Chapter 13, at least not right away. Instead, they chose to try to negotiate with their creditors. Their strategy was to convince the private creditors that they would be better off compromising on the amounts and payment terms rather than forcing the Wilsons into bankruptcy.

They are also negotiating with the IRS and their state tax agency. The Wilsons know that a major reduction in the amount owed is less likely than with a private creditor, but they have reason to believe that some compromise is possible.

They are not saving on legal fees. Several lawsuits are still pending, and each one has to be defended in court unless and until a definite deal is signed with the creditor involved. Also, they have decided to have a lawyer represent them in their dealings with the IRS.

Neither Chapter 7 nor Chapter 13 is permanently out of the question. Dave and Beth know that if they can't work out the deals they want or can't make the payment schedules agreed, they may still need to file for one or the other. Their lawyer has told them that they don't have to make a permanent decision. If their situation changes or they change their minds, they can file next week, next month, or next year.

For now, the Wilsons have decided that, except as an option held in reserve, neither Chapter 7 nor Chapter 13 is the solution for them.

CONCLUSION

Every day thousands of people across the country face the same kinds of financial decisions, and they are never pleasant. We hope that if you find yourself in such a situation, the information and suggestions in this book will help you reach the right solution for you.

STATE EXEMPTION LAWS

The following summaries describe *some* of the property that can be protected from creditors as exempt under the laws of each state, the District of Columbia, Puerto Rico, and the Virgin Islands.

In many states, the exemption laws are extensive and complicated. These are some of the highlights that apply in a relatively large number of cases. Many other provisions are omitted here or included in very general summaries.

To understand how the exemption laws work in a bankruptcy, read the main text of the book, especially the chapters on property, exempt property, and liens.

Alabama

Alabama residents *may not* choose the federal exemptions. They *must* use the state exemptions, including:

Many pension rights, insurance rights, and government benefits
Homestead, $5,000
Necessary wearing apparel
All books
Other personal property, $3,000

Alaska

Alaska's law makes it unclear whether residents may choose the federal exemptions. Also, the exemptions allowed to Alaskans in bankruptcy may be different from those allowed in a state court lawsuit. The exemptions apparently available are:

Many pension rights, insurance rights, and government benefits
Homestead, $54,000

Household goods, wearing apparel and books, $3,000
Jewelry, $1,000
Tools of trade, $2,800
Pets, $1,000
A motor vehicle, $3,000 in owner's equity and $20,000 total value
Liquor licenses
Some tenancy-by-the-entirety property

Arizona

Arizona residents *may not* choose the federal exemptions. They *must* use the state exemptions, including:

Many pension rights, insurance rights, and government benefits
Homestead, $100,000; special procedures must be followed
General household goods, $4,000
Bank account, $100;
Certain other household goods and items of personal property, in various amounts
Motor vehicle, $1,500; handicapped debtor, $4,000
Tools of trade, $2,500
Professionally prescribed health aids

Arkansas

Arkansas residents *may* choose the federal exemptions. They also have the option of using special state exemptions, including:

Many pension rights, insurance rights, and government benefits
Homestead, $2,500 in most cases;
Personal property, $500 for a head of household, $200 otherwise
Wearing apparel
Motor vehicle, $1,200
Wedding band, 1/2-carat diamond
Tools of trade, $750

California

California residents *may not* choose the federal exemptions. They may, however, choose between a set of state exemptions that are very similar to the federal exemptions and the standard state exemptions, including:

Many pension rights, insurance rights, and government benefits
Homestead:
• If debtor is part of family, $75,000
• If debtor is over 65 or disabled, $100,000
• Other debtors, $50,000
Reasonably necessary household goods
Jewelry, heirlooms, and works of art, $2,500

Reasonably necessary health aids
Tools of trade, $2,500
Motor vehicles, $1,200
Bank accounts or deposit accounts, $500 (one depositor) or $750 (two depositors)

Colorado
Colorado residents *may not* choose the federal exemptions. They *must* use the state exemptions, including:
Many pension rights, insurance rights, and government benefits
Homestead, $30,000
Necessary wearing apparel, $750
Jewelry, $500
Household goods, $1,500
Tools of trade, $1,500
Vehicle used in occupation, $1,000
Vehicle owned by person over 65 or handicapped, $3,000

Connecticut
Connecticut residents *may* choose the federal exemptions. They also have the option of using the state exemptions, including:
Many pension rights, insurance rights, and government benefits
Homestead, $75,000
Necessary apparel and household goods
Tools of trade
Motor vehicle, $1,500
Wedding and engagement rings

Delaware
Delaware residents *may not* choose the federal exemptions They *must* use the state exemptions, including:
Many pension rights, insurance rights, and government benefits
Wearing apparel
Personal property, $5,000
Some tenancy-by-the-entirety property

District of Columbia
District of Columbia residents *may* choose the federal exemptions. They also have the option of using District exemptions, including:
Many pension rights, insurance rights, and government benefits
Wearing apparel, $300
Household goods, $300
Tools of trade, $200
Motor vehicle, $500

Books, $400
Some tenancy-by-the-entirety property

Florida
Florida residents *may not* choose the federal exemptions. They *must* use the state exemptions, including:
Many pension rights, insurance rights, and government benefits
Homestead:
- In a municipality, ½ acre; special procedures are required
- Not in a municipality, 160 acres; special procedures are required
Personal property, $1,000
Some tenancy-by-the-entirety property

Georgia
Georgia residents *may not* choose the federal exemptions. Also, the exemptions allowed to Georgians in bankruptcy are different from those allowed in a state court lawsuit. They *must* use the state exemptions, including:
Many pension rights, insurance rights, and government benefits
Homestead, $5,000
Motor vehicles, $1,000
Household goods, $200 per item, $3,500 total
Jewelry, $500
Any property, $400 plus unused homestead exemption
Tools of trade, $500

Hawaii
Hawaii residents *may* choose the federal exemptions. They also have the option of using the state exemptions, including:
Many pension rights, insurance rights, and government benefits.
Homestead:
- Married, head of household, or over 65, $30,000
- Other persons, $20,000
Necessary household goods
Jewelry and watches, $1,000
Motor vehicle, $1,000
Tools of trade
Some tenancy-by-the-entirety property

Idaho
Idaho residents *may not* choose the federal exemptions. They *must* use the state exemptions, including:

Many pension rights, insurance rights, and government benefits
Homestead, $50,000
The following property, subject to a combined total of $4,000
• Necessary household goods
• One firearm
• Wearing apparel
Jewelry, $250
Tools of trade, $1,000
Motor vehicle, $1,500
Certain irrigation rights and growing crops

Illinois

Illinois residents *may not* choose the federal exemptions. They
must use the state exemptions, including:
Many pension rights, insurance rights, and government benefits
Homestead, $7,500
Necessary wearing apparel
Motor vehicle, $1,200
Tools of trade, $750
Any property, $2,000

Indiana

Indiana residents *may not* choose the federal exemptions. They
must use the state exemptions, including:
Many pension rights, insurance rights, and government benefits
Homestead, $7,500
"Tangible" personal property, $4,000
"Intangible" personal property, $100
Some tenancy-by-the-entirety property

Iowa

Iowa residents *may not* choose the federal exemptions. They *must*
use the state exemptions, including:
Many pension rights, insurance rights, and government benefits
Homestead:
• In a city or town, ½ acre
• Other, 40 acres
Wearing apparel, $1,000
Shotgun
Rifle
Books, $1,000
Household goods, $2,000
Cash or bank account, $100

The following property, subject to a combined total of $5,000:
* Musical instruments
* Motor vehicle
* Tax refunds, $1,000
Tools of trade, $10,000

Kansas

Kansas residents *may not* choose the federal exemptions. They *must* use the state exemptions, including:

Many pension rights, insurance rights, and government benefits
Homestead:
* In a city, 1 acre
* Farmland, 160 acres
Necessary furnishings
Jewelry, $1,000
One motor vehicle or means of transportation, used to get to work, $20,000
Motor vehicle equipped for handicapped person, no limit
Tools of trade, $7,500

Kentucky

Kentucky residents *may not* choose the federal exemptions. They *must* use the state exemptions, including:

Many pension rights, insurance rights, and government benefits
Homestead, $5,000 plus up to $1,000 unused personal property exemption
Household furnishings, jewelry, and clothing, $3,000
Motor vehicle:
* Personal, $2,500
* Business, $2,500
Tools of trade:
* Professional, $1,000
* Other, $300
Any property, $1,000

Louisiana

Louisiana residents *may not* choose the federal exemptions. They *must* use the state exemptions, including:

Many pension rights, insurance rights, and government benefits
Homestead, $15,000
Tools of trade
Nonluxury motor vehicle or truck weighing less than 3 tons if used in occupation
Books

Household goods
Wedding or engagement ring, $5,000

Maine

Maine residents *may not* choose the federal exemptions. They *must* use the state exemptions, including:

Many pension rights, insurance rights, and government benefits
Homestead, disabled or over 60, $60,000
Homestead, other, $12,500
Household goods, $200 per item
Jewelry, $750
Tools of trade, $5,000
Motor vehicle, $2,500
Implements necessary for farming
Commercial fisherman's boat, not exceeding 5 tons
Any property, $400
Additional household goods or tools of trade, up to $6,000 of any unused homestead exemption

Maryland

Maryland residents *may not* choose the federal exemptions. They *must* use the state exemptions, including:

Many pension rights, insurance rights, and government benefits
Tools of trade, $2,500
Household goods, $500
Any property (including homestead), $5,500
Some tenancy-by-the-entirety property

Massachusetts

Massachusetts residents *may* choose the federal exemptions. They also have the option of using the state exemptions, including:

Many pension rights, insurance rights, and government benefits
Homestead, $100,000
Homestead, disabled or over 65, $150,000
Necessary wearing apparel, beds, and heating unit
Household furniture, $3,000
Tools of trade, $500
Business inventory, $500
Automobile, $700
Savings account, $500
Some tenancy-by-the-entirety property

Michigan

Michigan residents *may* choose the federal exemptions. They also have the option of using the state exemptions, including:

Many pension rights, insurance rights, and government benefits
Homestead, $3,500
Wearing apparel
Household goods, $1,000
Tools of trade, $1,000
Some tenancy-by-the-entirety property

Minnesota

Minnesota residents *may* choose the federal exemptions. They also have the option of using the state exemptions, including:

Many pension rights, insurance rights, and government benefits
Homestead:
  * Within city, 1/2 acre; limited by court decision to amount reasonably necessary
  * Not in city, 80 acres; limited by court decision to amount reasonably necessary
Wearing apparel and household goods, $4,500
Tools of trade;
  * Farm, $13,000
  * Other, $5,000
Motor vehicle, $2,000

Mississippi

Mississippi residents *may not* choose the federal exemptions. They *must* use the state exemptions, including:

Many pension rights, insurance rights, and government benefits
Homestead, $30,000
Personal property, $10,000
Some tenancy-by-the-entirety property

Missouri

Missouri residents *may not* choose the federal exemptions. They *must* use the state exemptions, including:

Many pension rights, insurance rights, and government benefits
Homestead, $8,000
Household goods, $1,000
Jewelry, $500
Tools of trade, $2,000
Motor vehicle, $1,000
Any property, $400
Any property, head of family, additional $850, plus $250 for each dependent child under 18
Some tenancy-by-the-entirety property

Montana

Montana residents *may not* choose the federal exemptions. They *must* use the state exemptions, including:

Many pension rights, insurance rights, and government benefits

Homestead, $40,000

Household goods, wearing apparel, jewelry, and certain other property, $600 per item, $4,500 aggregate

Tools of trade, $3,000

Motor vehicle, $1,200

Nebraska

Nebraska residents *may not* choose the federal exemptions. They *must* use the state exemptions, including:

Many pension rights, insurance rights, and government benefits

Homestead, $10,000

Immediate personal possessions

Necessary wearing apparel

Household furniture and kitchen utensils, $1,500

Equipment or tools, $1,500

Personal property, persons without homestead, $2,500

Nevada

Nevada residents *may not* choose the federal exemptions. They *must* use the state exemptions, including:

Many pension rights, insurance rights, and government benefits

Homestead, $95,000

Necessary household goods, $3,000

Tools of trade, $4,500

Motor vehicle, $1,000

New Hampshire

New Hampshire residents *may not* choose the federal exemptions. They *must* use the state exemptions, including:

Many pension rights, insurance rights, and government benefits

Homestead, $30,000

Wearing apparel

Certain specified household goods

Household furniture, $2,000

Books, $800

Automobile, $1,000

Jewelry, $500

Tools of trade, $1,200

New Jersey

New Jersey residents *may* choose the federal exemptions. They also have the option of using the state exemptions, including:

Many pension rights, insurance rights, and government benefits
Wearing apparel
Household goods, $1,000
Any property, $1,000

New Mexico

New Mexico residents *may* choose the federal exemptions. They also have the option of using the state exemptions, including:

Many pension rights, insurance rights, and government benefits
Homestead, $30,000
Tools of trade, $1,500
Motor vehicle, $4,000
Jewelry, $2,500
Clothing
Furniture
Books
Any personal property, married person or head of household, $500
Any personal property other than money, single person, $500
Any property, person without homestead, $2,000

New York

New York residents *may not* choose the federal exemptions. They *must* use the state exemptions, including:

Many pension rights, insurance rights, and government benefits
Homestead, $10,000
Personal property, total $5,000, including:
• Wearing apparel, furniture, and appliances
• Wedding ring
• Tools of trade, $600
• Bank deposits (person without homestead), $2,500
Motor vehicle, $2,400
Some tenancy-by-the-entirety property

North Carolina

North Carolina residents *may not* choose the federal exemptions. They *must* use the state exemptions, including:

Many pension rights, insurance rights, and government benefits
Homestead, $7,500

Motor vehicle, $1,000

Household furnishings, $2,500 plus $500 for each dependent to maximum of $4,500

Tools of trade, $500

Any property, $2,500 less any amount applied to homestead exemption

Some tenancy-by-the-entirety property

North Dakota

North Dakota residents *may not* choose the federal exemptions. They *must* use the state exemptions, including:

Many pension rights, insurance rights, and government benefits.

Homestead, $80,000

Wearing apparel

Motor vehicle, $1,200

Any property:
- Head of household, $5,000, plus $7,500 if no homestead
- Single person, $2,500, plus $7,500 if no homestead

Ohio

Ohio residents *may not* choose the federal exemptions. They *must* use the state exemptions, including:

Many pension rights, insurance rights, and government benefits

Homestead, $5,000

Motor vehicle, $1,000

Bank account, $400

Household goods, jewelry, and money;
- Without homestead, $2,000
- With homestead, $1,500

Tools of trade, $750

Any property, $400

Some tenancy-by-the-entirety property

Oklahoma

Oklahoma residents *may not* choose the federal exemptions. They *must* use the state exemptions, including:

Many pension rights, insurance rights, and government benefits

Homestead;
- In city or town, up to ¼ acre
- Rural, up to 160 acres

Manufactured home used as homestead

Household furniture

Tools of trade

Wearing apparel, $4,000
Certain livestock
Motor vehicle, $3,000

Oregon

Oregon residents *may not* choose the federal exemptions. They *must* use the state exemptions, including:
Many pension rights, insurance rights, and government benefits
Homestead;
• One person, $25,000; or mobile home, $23,000
• Couple, $33,000; or mobile home, $30,000
Books, pictures, and musical instruments, $600
Wearing apparel, jewelry or personal items, $1,800
Tools of trade, $3,000
Vehicle, $1,700
One firearm
Household goods, $3,000

Pennsylvania

Pennsylvania residents *may* choose the federal exemptions. They also have the option of using the state exemptions, including:
Many pension rights, insurance rights, and government benefits
Wearing apparel
Any property, $300
Some tenancy-by-the-entirety property

Puerto Rico

Puerto Rico residents *may* choose the federal exemptions. They also have the option of using the commonwealth exemptions, including:
Many pension rights, insurance rights, and government benefits
Homestead, $1,500
Certain household goods
Wearing apparel
Water rights
Tools of trade, $300
Certain tools of trade of professionals
Motor vehicle used as tool of trade
Kitchen equipment
Washing machine, $200
Radio, $100
Television, $250

Rhode Island

Rhode Island residents *may* choose the federal exemptions. They also have the option of using the state exemptions, including:

Many pension rights, insurance rights, and government benefits
Wearing apparel
Tools of trade, $500
Household furniture, $1,000
Some tenancy-by-the-entirety property

South Carolina

South Carolina residents *may* choose the federal exemptions. They also have the option of using the state exemptions, including:

Many pension rights, insurance rights, and government benefits
Homestead, $5,000
Motor vehicle, $1,200
Household goods, $2,500
Jewelry, $500
Cash or liquid assets, persons without homestead, $1,000
Tools of trade, $750

South Dakota

South Dakota residents *may not* choose the federal exemptions. They *must* use the state exemptions, including:

Many pension rights, insurance rights, and government benefits
Homestead, $30,000
Homestead, over age 70, no limit
Books, $200
Wearing apparel
Any property;
• Head of household, $4,000
• Other, $2,000

Tennessee

Tennessee residents *may not* choose the federal exemptions. They *must* use the state exemptions, including:

Many pension rights, insurance rights, and government benefits
Homestead, $5,000
Wearing apparel
Tools of trade, $750
Any property, $4,000

Texas

Texas residents *may* choose the federal exemptions. They also have the option of using the state exemption, including:

Many pension rights, insurance rights, and government benefits.
Homestead;
- Urban, 1 acre
- Rural, 200 acres

Eligible personal property;
- Head of household, $60,000
- Single person, $30,000

Eligible personal property includes:
- Household goods
- Ranching or farming implements
- Clothing
- Athletic and sporting equipment
- Two vehicles

Tools of trade

Utah

Utah residents *may not* choose the federal exemptions. They *must* use the state exemptions, including:

Many pension rights, insurance rights, and government benefits

Homestead, $8,000 plus $2,000 for spouse and $500 for each other dependent

Certain specified household goods

Books and musical instruments, $500

Other furnishings, $500

Tools of trade, $1,500

One motor vehicle used as tool of trade, $1,500

Vermont

Vermont residents *may* choose the federal exemptions. They also have the option of using the state exemptions, including:

Many pension rights, insurance rights, and government benefits

Homestead, $30,000

Motor vehicles, $2,500

Wedding ring

Other jewelry, $500

Household furnishings, $2,500

Tools of trade, $5,000

Bank deposits, $700

Any other property, $5,000 to $7,000

Some tenancy-by-the-entirety property

Virgin Islands

Virgin Islands residents *may* choose the federal exemptions. They also have the option of using the territorial exemptions, including:

Many pension rights, insurance rights, and government benefits
Homestead, $30,000
Necessary wearing apparel
Tools of trade
Household goods, $3,000
Some tenancy-by-the-entirety property

Virginia
Virginia residents *may not* choose the federal exemptions. They *must* use the state exemptions, including:
Many pension rights, insurance rights, and government benefits
Homestead or personal property, $5,000 plus $500 for each dependent
Necessary wearing apparel
Certain specified household goods
Motor vehicles, $2,000
Tools of trade, $10,000
Some tenancy-by-the-entirety property

Washington
Washington residents *may* choose the federal exemptions. They also have the option of using the state exemptions, including:
Many pension rights, insurance rights, and government benefits
Homestead
Furs and jewelry, $1,000
Other wearing apparel
Household goods, $2,700
Any property, $1,000, but not more than $100 in cash, and $100 in savings, or securities
Motor vehicles, $2,500
Tools of trade, $5,000

West Virginia
West Virginia residents *may not* choose the federal exemptions. They *must* use the state exemptions, including:
Many pension rights, insurance rights, and government benefits
Homestead, $7,500
Motor vehicle, $1,200
Household goods, $200 per item, $1,000 total
Jewelry, $500
Tools of trade, $750
Any property, $400 plus unused homestead exemption

Wisconsin

Wisconsin residents *may* choose the federal exemptions. They also have the option of using the state exemptions, including:

Many pension rights, insurance rights, and government benefits

Homestead, $40,000

Business and farm property, $7,500

Personal property, $5,000

Motor vehicles, $1,200 plus unused personal property exemption

Depository accounts, $1,000

Wyoming

Wyoming residents *may not* choose the federal exemptions. They *must* use the state exemptions, including:

Many pension rights, insurance rights, and government benefits

Homestead, $10,000

Necessary wearing apparel, $1,000

Household goods, $2,000

Motor vehicles, $2,000

Tools of trade, $2,000

Some tenancy-by-the-entirety property

FEDERAL BANKRUPTCY STATUTES

The following are key portions of the federal Bankruptcy Code, Section 522(d), which lists the exempt property available to bankruptcy petitioners in many states, and Section 523(a), which lists the categories of debts that are not canceled by a Chapter 7 discharge of debts. Cross-references to other statutes are omitted.

§522. Exemptions

(a)–(c) [omitted]
(d) The following property may be exempted [by petitioners in states that allow use of the federal exemptions]:
  (1) The debtor's aggregate interest, not to exceed $15,000 in value, in real property or personal property that the debtor or a dependent of the debtor uses as a residence, in a cooperative that owns property that the debtor or a dependent of the debtor uses as a residence, or in a burial plot for the debtor or a dependent of the debtor.
  (2) The debtor's interest, not to exceed $2,400 in value, in one motor vehicle.
  (3) The debtor's interest, not to exceed $400 in value in any particular item or $8,000 in aggregate value, in household furnishing, household goods, wearing apparel, appliances, books, animals, crops, or musical instruments, that are held primarily for the personal, family, or household use of the debtor or a dependent of the debtor.
  (4) The debtor's aggregate interest, not to exceed $1,000 in

value, in jewelry held primarily for the personal, family, or household use of the debtor or a dependent of the debtor.

(5) The debtor's aggregate interest in any property, not to exceed in value $800 plus up to $7,500 of any unused amount of the exemption provided under paragraph (1) of this subsection.

(6) The debtor's aggregate interest, not to exceed $1,500 in any implements, professional books, or tools, of the trade of the debtor or the trade of dependent of the debtor.

(7) Any unmatured life insurance contract owned by the debtor, other than a credit life insurance contract.

(8) The debtor's aggregate interest, not to exceed in value $8,000 . . . in any accrued dividend or interest under, or loan value of, any unmatured life insurance contract owned by the debtor under which the insured is the debtor or an individual of whom the debtor is a dependent.

(9) Professionally prescribed health aids for the debtor or a dependent of the debtor.

(10) The debtor's right to receive:
   (A) a social security benefit, unemployment compensation, or a local public assistance benefit;
   (B) a veterans' benefit;
   (C) a disability, illness, or unemployment benefit;
   (D) alimony, support or separate maintenance, to the extent reasonably necessary for the support of the debtor, and any dependent of the debtor;
   (E) a payment under a stock bonus, pension, profitsharing, annuity, or similar plan or contract on account of illness, disability, death, age, or length of service, to the extent reasonably necessary for the support of the debtor and any dependent of the debtor, unless—
      (i) such plan or contract was established by or under the auspices of an insider that employed the debtor at the time the debtor's rights under such plan or contract arose;
      (ii) such payment is on account of age or length of service; and
      (iii) such plan or contract does not qualify under [certain sections of the Internal Revenue Code].

(11) The debtor's right to receive, or property that is traceable to—

(A) an award under a crime victim's reparation law;

(B) a payment on account of the wrongful death of an individual of whom the debtor was a dependent, to the extent reasonably necessary for the support of the debtor and any dependent of the debtor;

(C) a payment under a life insurance contract that insured the life of an individual of whom the debtor was a dependent on the date of such individual's death, to the extent reasonably necessary for the support of the debtor and any dependent of the debtor;

(D) a payment, not to exceed $15,000, on account of personal bodily injury, not including pain and suffering or compensation or actual pecuniary loss, of the debtor or an individual of whom the debtor is a dependent; or

(E) a payment in compensation of loss of future earnings of the debtor or an individual of whom the debtor is or was a dependent, to the extent reasonably necessary for the support of the debtor and any dependent of the debtor.

§523. Exceptions to discharge

(a) A discharge under [Chapter 7 or Chapter 13] does not discharge an individual debtor from any debt—

(1) for a tax or a customs duty—

(A) of the kind and for the periods [that entitle a debt to priority under] this title, whether or not a claim for such tax was filed or allowed;

(B) with respect to which a return, if required—

(i) was not filed; or

(ii) was filed after the date on which return was last due, under applicable law or under any extension, and after two years before the date of the filing of the petition; or

(C) with respect to which the debtor made a fraudulent return or willfully attempted in any manner to evade or defeat such tax;

(2) for money, property, services, or an extension, renewal, or refinancing of credit, to the extent obtained by—

(A) false pretenses, a false representation, or actual fraud, other than a statement respecting the debtor's or an insider's financial condition;

(B) use of a statement in writing—
  (i) that is materially false;
  (ii) respecting the debtor's or an insider's financial condition;
  (iii) on which the creditor to whom the debtor is liable for such money, property, services, or credit reasonably relied; and
  (iv) that the debtor caused to be made or published with intent to deceive; or

(C) for purposes of subparagraph (A) of this paragraph, consumer debts owed to a single creditor and aggregating more than $1,000 for "luxury goods or services" incurred by an individual debtor on or within 60 days before the order for relief under this title, or cash advances aggregating more than $1,000 that are extensions of consumer credit under an open end credit plan obtained by an individual debtor on or within twenty days before the order for relief under this title, are presumed to be nondischargeable; "luxury goods or services" do not include goods or services reasonably acquired for the support or maintenance of the debtor or a dependent of the debtor . . . ;

(3) neither listed nor scheduled [in the bankruptcy documents], with the name, if known to the debtor, of the creditor to whom such debt is owed, in time to permit—

(A) if such debt is not of a kind specified in paragraph (2), (4), or (6) of this subsection, timely filing of a proof of claim, unless such creditor had notice or actual knowledge of the case in time for such timely filing;

(B) if such debt is of a kind specified in paragraph (2), (4), or (6) of this subsection, timely filing of a proof of claim and timely request for a determination of dischargeability of such debt under one of such paragraphs, unless such creditor had notice or actual knowledge of the case in time for such timely filing and request;

(4) for fraud or defalcation while acting in a fiduciary capacity, embezzlement, or larceny;

(5) to a spouse, former spouse, or child of the debtor, for alimony to, maintenance for, or support of such spouse or

child, in connection with a separation agreement, divorce decree or other order of a court of record, determination made in accordance with state or territorial law by a government unit, or property settlement agreement, but not to the extent that—

(A) such debt is assigned to another entity, voluntarily, by operation of law, or otherwise (other than debts assigned [for public assistance reimbursement under] the Social Security Act, or any such debt which has been assigned to the Federal Government or to a State or any political subdivision of such State); or

(B) such debt includes a liability designated as alimony, maintenance, or support, unless such liability is actually in the nature of alimony, maintenance, or support;

(6) for willful and malicious injury by the debtor to another entity or to the property of another entity;

(7) to the extent such debt is for a fine, penalty, or forfeiture payable to and for the benefit of a governmental unit, and is not compensation for actual pecuniary loss, other than a tax penalty—

(A) relating to a tax of a kind not specified in paragraph (1) of this subsection; or

(B) imposed with respect to a transaction or event that occurred before three years before the date of the filing of the petition;

(8) for an educational benefit overpayment or loan made, insured or guaranteed by a governmental unit, or made under any program funded in whole or in part by a governmental unit or nonprofit institution, or for an obligation to repay funds received as an educational benefit, scholarship or stipend, unless—

(A) such loan first became due more than 7 years (exclusive of any applicable suspension of the repayment period) before the date of the filing of the petition; or

(B) excepting such debt from discharge under this paragraph will impose an undue hardship on the debtor and the debtor's dependents;

(9) for death or personal injury caused by the debtor's operation of a motor vehicle if such operation was unlawful because the debtor was intoxicated from using alcohol, a drug, or another substance; or

(10) that was or could have been listed or scheduled by the

debtor in a prior case concerning the debtor under this title or under the Bankruptcy Act in which the debtor waived discharge, or was denied a discharge . . .;

(11) [certain fraud claims with respect to a depository institution or credit union];

(12) [certain other claims relating to management of depository institutions].

(13) for any payment of an order of restitution issued under title 18, United States Code;

(14) incurred to pay a tax to the United States that would be nondischargeable pursuant to paragraph (1);

(15) not of the kind described in paragraph (5) that is incurred by the debtor in the course of a divorce or separation or in connection with a separation agreement, divorce decree or other order of a court of record, a determination made in accordance with State or territorial law by a governmental unit unless—

   (A) the debtor does not have the ability to pay such debt from income or property of the debtor not reasonably necessary to be expended for the maintenance or support of the debtor or a dependent of the debtor and, if the debtor is engaged in a business, for the payment of expenditures necessary for the continuation, preservation, and operation of such business; or

   (B) discharging such debt would result in a benefit to the debtor that outweighs the detrimental consequences to a spouse, former spouse, or child of the debtor;

(16) for a fee or assessment that becomes due and payable after the order for relief to a membership association with respect to the debtor's interest in a dwelling unit that has condominium ownership or in a share of a cooperative housing corporation, but only if such fee or assessment is payable for a period during which—

   (A) the debtor physically occupied a dwelling unit in the condominium or cooperative project; or

   (B) the debtor rented the dwelling unit to a tenant and received payments from the tenant for such period,

but nothing in this paragraph shall except from discharge the debt of a debtor for a membership association fee or assessment for a period arising before entry of the order for relief in a pending or subsequent bankruptcy case.

GLOSSARY OF TERMS

The following terms are used in this book. Italicized terms in definitions are themselves defined in other entries.

Accelerate   As used in reference to an installment loan, to make the entire amount due immediately, rather than in a series of separate payments. *Creditors* often accelerate loans if payments are missed.

Accounts receivable   Money owed to a business by its customers, but not yet paid.

Automatic stay   Court order caused by filing a bankruptcy petition under any chapter. The automatic stay halts nearly all debt collection activity against the petitioner by creditors, including lawsuits.

Bankruptcy   Legal procedure for dealing with debt problems, specifically a case filed under one of the chapters of Title 11 of the United States Code (the Bankruptcy Code).

Bankruptcy estate   Legal structure set up for each bankruptcy case that takes over ownership of the petitioner's property. In many *Chapter 7* cases, the rights of the bankruptcy estate are only temporary and the petitioner never loses control of any of his or her property.

Bankruptcy trustee   Official appointed in all *Chapter 7* and *Chapter 13* cases to represent the rights of the creditors. In a Chapter 7 case, the *trustee* determines whether the *petitioner* has any property that can legally be sold for the benefit of *creditors.* In a Chapter 13 case, the trustee often makes a recommendation on whether the debt repayment plan should be approved, receives the payments from the petitioner, and pays the money out to creditors.

Chapter 7 Section of the federal Bankruptcy Code that provides for outright cancellation of most types of personal debts without a repayment plan and for possible sale of some types of property to pay such debts.

Chapter 11 Section of the federal Bankruptcy Code that provides for financial reorganization of businesses.

Chapter 12 Section of the federal Bankruptcy Code that provides for financial reorganization of family farms.

Chapter 13 Section of the federal Bankruptcy Code that provides for adjustment of the debts of an individual with regular income. Chapter 13 allows individuals to repay their debts in full or to pay part and discharge the rest, while receiving protection from creditors.

Collateral Property put up by a borrower as security for a loan. See also *lien*.

Complaint Document in a lawsuit that notifies the court and the *defendant* of the grounds claimed by the *plaintiff* for an award of money or other court order against the defendant.

Confirmation In a *Chapter 13* or other bankruptcy debt reorganization or adjustment case, the process by which the judge approves a debt repayment plan.

Contingent debt Debt that may be owed under certain circumstances, such as if you are cosigner of another person's loan and that person fails to pay it off.

Corporation Type of organization set up under state law and often used to own and operate businesses. For many purposes, a corporation is legally treated as if it were a separate person. The owner or owners of a corporation are protected from having to pay some types of corporate debts even if the corporation does not pay.

Creditor Person or business to which money is owed for any reason or that claims that money is owed to it.

Credit rating General term for a person's creditworthiness. Lenders and other *creditors* usually base their decisions primarily on the applicant's present income, other debts, and assets.

Credit report Report prepared by an credit agency or bureau, showing certain financial data, usually about an applicant for a loan or job.

Debtor Person who owes or is claimed to owe money to another person or business for any reason; also, the official term for a person who files a petition under any chapter of the Bankruptcy Code.

Defendant   Person or business against which a lawsuit is filed.

Dischargeable debt   Debt that can legally be canceled in a bankruptcy. Certain categories of debts, including most taxes and recent student loans, are *not* dischargeable. Some *secured debts* are protected from being discharged for all practical purposes because the petitioner must continue to pay the debt or lose the collateral.

Discharge of debts   Court order in a bankruptcy case that declares that certain categories of the petitioner's debts are canceled and forbids creditors to make any future attempt to collect them.

Encumbered property   Property that is subject to a *lien* or that has been used as *collateral* for a loan.

Equity   As used in connection with bankruptcy, equity usually means the value of an owner's interest in property, after deducting *liens*. If a home that could be sold for $60,000 is subject to a mortgage of $40,000 but no other liens, the owner has equity of $20,000 in the home.

Exemption planning   Transactions by which a *debtor* buys, sells, or otherwise deals with his or her property to take better advantage of *exempt property* laws.

Exempt property   As used in connection with bankruptcy, property or value in property is exempt when a petitioner is allowed to keep it, free from the claims of *creditors* who do not have *liens*.

Foreclosure   Legal procedure by which a *creditor* enforces a *lien*; usually applied to real estate *mortgages*. See also *repossession*.

Joint petitioners   As used in bankruptcy law, a husband and wife who file a bankruptcy petition together.

Judgment   Order or decision of a court, particularly an award in favor of a party that has won a lawsuit. A judgment that declares that money is owed is a *money judgment*.

Judgement lien   *Lien* in property that belongs to a *debtor,* created in favor of a *creditor* that has sued and won a *money judgment*.

Judicial lien   *Lien* awarded to a *creditor* by a court, such as when a creditor has filed a lawsuit over an uncollected debt and won.

Junior lien   *Lien* that can be paid out of the value of the *collateral* only after another (senior) lien that takes precedence is paid off.

Lien   Special right or interest of a *creditor* in property to assure that the debt owed it is paid. Real estate *mortgages* and automobile loans secured by a car are common examples of liens.

Limited liability   Legal rule under which the owners of an incorporated business cannot be forced to pay some kinds of debts of the *corporation,* even if the corporation fails to pay.

Limited liability company   A legal structure similar to a *corporation* that is treated like a *partnership* for some tax purposes

Limited partnership   A type of *partnership* in which some limited partners have legal rights similar to stockholders in a *corporation,* and are not personally liable for most business debts.

Meeting of creditors   Court hearing held at the beginning of a bankruptcy case, at which the *trustee* and *creditors* can question the *petitioner.*

Money judgment   Court *judgment* awarding money.

Mortgage   *Lien* voluntarily given by the owner of property to a *creditor;* most commonly used with regard to homes or other real estate.

Partnership   A business structure with two or more owners. Unlike stockholders in a *corporation,* general partners are liable for all partnership debts.

Petitioner   One who files a petition, including the petition to the court that starts a bankruptcy case.

Plaintiff   Person or business that files a lawsuit.

Plan   As used in bankruptcy, terms stated by a *petitioner* in a *Chapter 13* case or other reorganization by which the petitioner intends to pay off some or all debts.

Property   Anything of monetary value, including land, investments, household goods, etc.

Reaffirmation agreement   Agreement by a *Chapter 7* bankruptcy *petitioner* to continue paying a debt after the bankruptcy, usually for the purpose of keeping *collateral* or mortgaged property that would otherwise be subject to *repossession.*

Real estate   Land or buildings.

Replevin   Legal term for *repossession.*

Repossession   Procedure by which a *creditor* attempts to obtain possession of *property* that has been pledged to it as *collateral.* Repossession usually requires court action but may not in some cases, particularly auto repossession.

Secured debt   Debt that is backed by a *mortgage,* pledge of *collateral,* or other *lien.*

Security interest   *Lien* created by agreement between the *debtor* and *creditor,* as distinguished from a lien created by a court or by automatic application of a law.

Senior lien   *Lien* that ranks ahead of other liens on the same *property* and is entitled to be paid first if the property is sold or *foreclosed*. For example, a purchase *mortgage* taken out when a house is bought is senior to a second mortgage later taken out on the same house.

Sole proprietorship   A business owned by one person that is not incorporated.

Statement of intention   Declaration made by a *Chapter 7 petitioner* concerning plans for dealing with *secured debts*.

Statutory lien   *Lien* created by statute; that is, by law without need for either an agreement or court action. Tax liens are a common example of statutory liens.

Stay   Court order that something not be done. See also *automatic stay.*

Stockholder   Someone who holds shares of stock, or ownership rights, in a *corporation.*

Summons   Court document that tells someone to appear in court or file a written answer to a lawsuit. In lawsuits for money, the summons is usually delivered with a *complaint* that states the reason for the lawsuit.

Tax lien   *Lien* obtained by a government tax authority on *property* of a person with overdue tax obligations.

Tenancy by the entirety   (or entireties) Type of joint ownership in *property* between husband and wife in some states. Property held in this type of ownership sometimes has special protection from *creditors.*

Trustee   Someone who controls *property* in a trust for the benefit of someone else. See also *bankruptcy trustee* and *bankruptcy estate.*

Unliquidated debt   Debt, the amount of which is not yet known or determinable by simple arithmetic, such as an unresolved claim for personal injury

Unmatured debt   Debt that is not yet due, such as future payments on an installment account.

Unscheduled debt   Debt that should have been listed by a bankruptcy petitioner on the list of *creditors* filed with the court but was not. Depending on the circumstances, an unscheduled debt may or may not be excluded from a *discharge of debts.*

Wage earner bankruptcy   (or wage earner plan) Obsolete term for a *Chapter 13* debt adjustment case.

Wage garnishment   Legal procedure by which a *creditor* who has won a lawsuit against a wage earner can have the employer ordered to send part of the wage earner's pay directly to the creditor to pay on the debt.

Wild card exemption   Law that allows a person to protect from seizure by *creditors* a certain dollar amount of any *property* of his or her choice, rather than property in a specific category. See also *exempt property*.